Just Published,
BOERHAAVE's
Method of Studying PHYSICK.

Containing what a Physician ought to know in Relation to the Nature of Bodies, the Laws of Motion; *Staticks, Hydrostaticks, Hydraulicks*, and the Proprieties of Fluids: *Chymistry, Pharmacy* and *Botany*: *Osteology, Myology, Splanchnology, Angiology* and *Dissection*: The Theory and Practice of Physick: *Physiology, Pathology, Surgery, Diet*, &c. And the whole *Praxis Medica Interna*; with the Names and Characters of the most excellent Authors on all these several Subjects in every Age: *Systematicks, Observators, Operators*, &c. their best Editions, and the Method of reading them. Written in *Latin* by the Learned HERMAN BOERHAVE, Now Professor of Physick in the University of *Leyden*. Translated into English by *Mr.* Samber. Price Five Shillings.

Medicum creavit Altissimus. Altissimus creavit de Terra Medicinam. Eccles. cap. 38.

Printed for *C. Rivington*, at the *Bible* and *Crown* in St. *Paul*'s Church-Yard: *B. Creake* in *Jermyn-Street*, St. *James*'s; And *J. Sackfield* in *Lincolns-Inn-Square*.

A SYSTEM OF Experimental Philosophy, Prov'd by MECHANICKS.

WHEREIN

The *Principles* and *Laws* of *Physicks*, *Mechanicks*, *Hydrostaticks*, and *Opticks*, are demonstrated and explained at large, by a great Number of curious Experiments: With a full Description of the *Air-Pump*, and the several Experiments thereon: As also of the different Species of *Barometers*, *Thermometers*, and *Hydrometers*; as shewn at the publick Lectures in a Course of *Mechanical* and *Experimental Philosyphy*. As performed

By J. T. Desaguliers. M. A. F. R S.

Illustrated with several Copper Plates.

To which is added,

Sir *Isaac Newton*'s Colours: The Description of the condensing *Engine*, with its *Apparatus*: And Rowley's HORARY; a *Machine* representing the Motion of the *Moon* about the *Earth*; *Venus* and *Mercury* about the *Sun*, according to the *Copernican* SYSTEM.

LONDON:

Printed for B. Creake, at the *Bible and Ink-Bottle* in *Jermyn-Street*, St. *James*'s: J. Sackfield, in *Lincolns-Inn-Square*: And Sold by W. Mears, at the *Lamb* without *Temple-Bar* 1719.

Price Five Shillings.

T O

Sir Richard Steele.

SIR,

YOUR continual Care of me from my Infant Years has been so remarkably Generous, that I should be guilty of the deepest Ingrati-
tude

The DEDICATION.

tude in the World, did I not lay hold of all Occasions of acknowledging the many and great Obligations I have to you.

I therefore humbly Present to You the following *Treatise,* containing the several *Philosophical Experiments* shewn by Mr. *Desaguliers* in his publick *Lectures,* which I have carefully collected, and that *Gentleman* approved of.

The Dedication.

A Work so Curious cannot fail to give extream Pleasure and Satisfaction to all *Gentlemen* who are Lovers of the most useful Part of *Philosophy*, [the Experimental] especially those who have been present at these Courses of Mr. *Desaguliers*, as I my self have constantly been.

But as my successful going through these Courses, has been

The DEDICATION.

been entirely owing to Your Munificence and Bounty, so I know of no one who has so great a Right to this *Treatise* as Your Self, from whose Generosity it derived its Being.

It flys then to You for Protection, who have merited so much from Mankind; and whose NAME will shine for ever Bright amongst those of the BELLE LETTRE: This will be an Honour to Mr. DE-

The DEDICATION.

DESAGULIERS, whose Experiments they are; but particularly so to,

SIR,

Your most obedient,

and most faithful Servant,

PAUL DAWSON.

THE
CONTENTS.

HE *Definition of* NATURAL PHILOSOPHY, *and its first Principles.* From Page 1. to Page 12.

MECHANICAL EXPERIMENTS. 12.

MECHANICAL POWERS, *and their Definitions.* 21.

Suppositions. 22.

The Contents.

Axioms.   p. 23.

How to make a heavy Body seem to rise it self.   24.

SCHOLIUM.   25.

Of the BALANCE.   27.

Of the LEAVER.   31.

Of the PULLEY.   37.

Of the AXLE *in the* WHEEL.   39.

Of the WEDGE.   40.

SCHOLIUM.   43.

Of the SCREW.   44.

SCHOLIUM.   46.

The Contents.

Of the LAWS *of* NATURE.   p. 47.

HYDROSTATICHS.   74.

Definitions and Experiments.   From 74 to 122.

A Description of the AIR-PUMP *Mr.* BOYLE *made use of.*   122.

Experiments of the AIR-PUMP.   128.

How to Condense the AIR, *so that you may put what Quantity you please into a Vessel.*   133.

Of BAROMETERS, THERMOMETERS, *and* HYDROMETERS.   134.

CATOP.

The Contents.

CATOPTRICHS. p. 147.

Definitions. ibid.

DIOPTRICHS. 155.

Sir Isaac Newton's COLOURS. p. 187.

A DESCRIPTION of the Condensing ENGINE with its Apparatus. 192.

A DESCRIPTION of ROWLEY's HORARY, being a Machine to repre-

The Contents.

represent the Motion *of the* Moon *about the* Earth, *and the* Earth, Venus *and* Mercury *about the* Sun. p. 194.

A

LECTURES
OF
Experimental PHILOSOPHY.

WHEREIN

The Principles of *Mechanicks*, *Hydrostaticks*, and *Opticks*, are Demonstrated and Explained at large, by a great Number of curious Experiments: With a Description of the Air-Pump, and the several Experiments thereon: Of the Condensing-Engine; as also of the different Species of *Barometers*, *Thermometers*, and *Hygrometers*; with several Experiments to prove and explain Sir ISAAC NEWTON's *Theory of Light and Colours*, as performed in a Course of MECHANICAL and EXPERIMENTAL PHILOSOPHY.

By J. T. DESAGULIERS, *M. A. F. R. S.*

Illustrated with several curious Copper Plates suitable to each Subject.

To which is added,

A DESCRIPTION of Mr. *Rowley*'s Machine, called the ORRERY, which represents the Motion of the *Moon* about the *Earth*, *Venus* and *Mercury* about the *Sun*, according to the *Copernican System*: All carefully Examined and Corrected by Mr. *Desaguliers*.

The SECOND EDITION.

LONDON:

Printed for W. MEARS, at the *Lamb* without *Temple-Bar*; B. CREAKE, at the *Bible* in *Jermyn-Street*, St. *James's*; and J. SACKFIELD in *Lincolns-Inn-Square*. MDCCXIX.

Price Five Shillings.

PREFACE,

OR

Advertisement to the READER.

By J. T. Desaguliers, *M. A.* &c.

I *Think my self obliged to give an Account of the following Lectures, to serve as an Apology for their appearing before I designed to publish them.*

It is about sixteen or seventeen Years since Dr. John Keil (the present Savilian Professor of Astronomy) first gave Courses of Ex-

The PREFACE.

perimental Philosophy in Oxford; and being desired by some of his Auditors to give them something in Writing upon that Subject, he wrote a few Papers to serve them as Memorandums. I was his Scholar at the last Course he gave before he went beyond Sea; but could not then get those Papers. Some time after he was gone, I was desired by some of my Friends (who knew that I had applied my self to Experimental Philosophy) to give publick Courses, and then my Auditors desired to have written Lectures. I endeavoured to get Dr. Keil's Lectures, (as they were called) which when they were brought me I found altered according to the Fancy and Number of the Transcribers. Some Papers relating to Motion seem'd to be translated from Sir Isaac Newton's Principia, the Optical Lectures from Dr. Gregory's Catoptricks, and some of the Hydrostatical Propositions I took to be

The Preface.

be put in the Method in which they were by Dr. Keil. I then corrected the Faults, added other Propositions so as to make the Book as big again as before, that it might agree with the Lectures I then gave, and drew ten Tables of Figures which I got engraven in Copper Plates, that every Auditor that was at the Pains to transcribe the Lectures, might have an Impression of the Plates, to save himself the Trouble of drawing the Figures. Mr. Dawson (a young Man whom Sir Richard Steel had put under my Care) took a Copy of the Lectures above-mentioned, that they might be of Service to him when he went thro' my Courses, and they were afterwards sold and published without my Knowledge. But as the Booksellers have made me Satisfaction, and purchased the Copy of me, I have looked over the whole Book, and corrected every Error therein; because I was unwilling that those who buy

The Preface.

buy it should find it any wise imperfect, and desirous that it might be of use to such as go thro' Courses of Experimental Philosophy.

The Reader therefore is desired to correct the Faults with his Pen, as the Errata direct, before he begins to read the Lectures.

ERRATA.

ERRATA.

PAg. 7. Lin. 3. r. *Ingredients.* l. 21. r. *or coeval.* p. 8. l. 10. r. *Matter at first pull'd.* p. 14. r. *to weigh twelve.* p. 17. l. 19. r. *Fulcrum* B C. p. 18. l. 19. r. *one Pound at* A *will sustain.* p. 19. l. 19. dele *not* p. 22. l. 1. r. *fix'd Point.* p. 24. l. 7. r. *Piece, as* D. l. 8. r. C C. *at the other End bearing on two Pieces that are higher.* l. 10. r. *radius of the Body.* p. 30. l. 4. r. *lance is to the Weight of the Ballance.* p. 31. l. 4. r. *Weight of.* p. 33. l. 15. r. *fix'd Point.* p. 34. l. 8. dele K E G. p. 42. l. 23. r. G O *the Velocity.* l. ult. r. *to* G F. p. 43. l. 2. r. E F O & G O *which.* p. 44. r. *pondus, and of.* l. 16. dele *of the second kind.* p. 45. l. 6. dele L. l. 10. r. *Power must be to.* l. 18. r. *Helices.* l. 19. r. *Velocity.* l. 22 r. *is longer.* p. 47. l. 7 & 8. r. *an endless Screw.* p. 53. l. 21. r. *pushed (by.* l. 22. r. *Force) towards.* p. 54. l. 1. r. *the Force impress'd.* l. 3. r. *double Momentum, or Quantity of Motion.* p. 55. l. 13. dele *with.* l. 17. r. *times. When.* ibid. dele (;) after *descends.* l. 23. r. *instant of time, as the.* p. 56. l. 7. dele *with.* l. 11. r. *as the times.* p. 62. l. 1. r. *Motion.* l. 13. r. *upon* A *in the Direction* C A. p. 63. l. 20. r. B *comes to* A. l. 21. r. *the Boat* A. p. 65. l. 14. r. *forwards, it.* p. 72. l. 12. r. *towards each other with.* p. 82. l. ult. dele K E D. p. 84. l. 7. r. *above the Superficies.* p. 86. l. 11. r. *exceeds.* l. 17. r. *immediately over.* l. 19. r. *to be nearly.* l. ult. r. *to press above.* p. 87. l. ult. r. *Prisms or Columns.* p. 88. l. 1. after B r. F. l. 11. r. *exactly fitted.* l. 13. r. *Sides of the Cylinder, let a* E *be.* p. 90. l. 15. & 91. l. 6. dele K E D. p. 96. l. 17. r. *mount.* l. ult. r. *exceeded by it.* ibid. for *Surface* r. *Height.* ibid. f. *would* r. *when they would.* p. 97. l. 3. r. *immers'd.* f. *heavier* r. *lighter.* l. 9. r. *is to the.* l. 14. dele *to.* l. 15. dele K E D. p. 100. l. 5. r. E A D F. p. 103. l. 12. r. *will continue.* l. 22 & 23. r. *after having pump'd out the Air.* p. 104. l. 11. r. *external.* l. 21. r. *of* 28, 29, *or* 30 *Inches.* l. ult. r. *less than* 28 *Inches.* p. 105. l. 10. r. C P. *will be.* l. 11. r. C *shall sustain.* l. 22 & 23. r. *as before, is Gravity acting partly.* p. 106. l. 1. r. *depends.* l. 11 & 12. r. *of* 28 *or* 30 *Inches.* p. 107. l. penult. f. *is* r. *would.* before *to* r. *be.* p. 108. l. 7 & 8. r. 29 *or* 30 *Inches.* l. 10, 11, 12. *remain at* 28, 29, 30, *or* 31 *Inches* p. 109. l. 10. r. *the different Gravity of the Air, and therefore foretells foul or fair Weather.* p. 111. l. 13. r. *longer Tube more than in the shorter.* l. 17. r. *recurved Tube.* p. 113. at the end of l. 2. add, *That shews that Pillars of Air of equal Basis and equal Heights balance one another.* l. 3. r. ☿ *will rise by sucking it thro' a Crane or Syphon, but not.* l. 4. r. *Height as Water.* l. 17. r. *restitutive.* p. 117. l. 3. r. *restitutive.* p. 118. after *last line*, r. *if they be let down too suddenly.* p. 120. l. 1. r. *Tube.* p. 121. l. 16. r. *the Syringe is left.* p. 122. l. 5. r. *made use of it (but according to the Alterations that I have made in it since it has been in my Possession.)* p. 124. f. *Cleft* r. *Close.* p. 125. l. 19. f. *left* r. *soft.* l. 23. r. *let the soft Leather.* l. 24. r. *that by the Pressure.* l. ult. dele *the more.* p. 129 l. 7. r. *hanging a Weight.* p. 130. l. 6. r. *will not subside.* l. 12. r. *flaccid Bladder.* p. 134. l. 5. r. *the Cock.* l. 9. r. *Hygrometers.* p. 135. l. 8. r. *fitted.* l. 10. r. 31 *Inches.* l. 11. r. *at* 30, *sometimes at* 29. l. 12. dele *sometimes it will sink to* 27. l. 15 & 16. r. *to the Quantity of Matter, it is.* p. 136. l. 10. f. *Society* r. *Academy.* l. 13. f. *in* r. *on.* p. 139. l. 1. f. *String*

ERRATA.

f. *String* r. *Chain.* p. 143. l. 11 & 12. r. *highly rectified.* p. 145. l. 2. r. *nice Balance.* p. 149. l. 6. f. *vertical* r. *virtual.* p. 150. l. 7. r. *to a* B. l. 11. r. *the Angles* B D *a.* p. 151. l. 23 & 24. r. E F, *and form an Image behind it, and this.* p. 153. l. 2. r. *before the Glass.* p. 156. l. 7 & 8. r. *the Angle of Refraction,* l. 20. r. *if the Light.* p. 157. l. penult. r. *the Perpendicular, in the Line* H E. p. 158. l. 3. r. *towards* D, *and.* l. 7. r. *which is.* l. 14. f. *therein* r. *thereof.* p. 159. l. 14. f. *Divergence* r. *Convergence.* l. 20. r. *a Line parallel to the.* p. 160. l. 21. r. *be successively at* a, b, *and* c, *it will.* p. 162. l. ult. r. *greater in Proportion to its Distance from the Eye than.* p. 165. l. 11. r. *from* A *will enter.* ibid. f. *if* r. *as if they.* l. 18. r. *at* b *a nearer.* p. 166. l. 4. *after called* r. *the Iris of the Eye, which is part of the Uvea.* l. 5. f. *as* r. *is.* l. 16. dele *by.* p. 171. l. 1. r. *Angle* a C b. l. 6. f. *of* r. *at.* l. 17. f. *lie* r. *see.* p. 178. l. 6. f. *Concave* r. *Convex.* l. 11. r. *which is seen under a greater Angle.* p. 181. r. α β instead of *a b* throughout the whole Page. p. 182. l. 1. r. *is greater.* l. 4. r. α β. l. 11. f. *under* r. *on.* l. 12. r. *the Eye subtends the same Angle as* A B. l. 14. r. *is as* K. l. 20. r. *as* α β. l. 21. r. α E β. p. 183. r. α β instead of *a b* throughout the whole Page. p. 184. l. 6. f. *Convex* r. *Concave.* l. 9, 10, 17. r. α β for *a b.* l. 18. f. *vertical* r. *virtual.* p. 185. l. 1. r. *to* α β. l. 4. r. *to* α F β. l. 5. r. *the Image* α β. l. 8. & 11. f. *virtical* r. *virtual.* p. 186. l. 9. dele *a b.* l. 12. before *Image* r. *last,* dele *a b.* l. 13, 14. r. *Point of it may enter.* l. 20, 21. r. *and the last Image is in the.* p. 188. l. 16. r. *the Glass, as in Figure* 3. l. 21. r. *Fig.* 2. p. 189. l. 10. f. *it* r. *the first Prism next the Window refract.* l. 22 & 24. f. *refracted on* r. *reflected by.* p. 190. l. 1. r. *particular Colour.* l. 9. f. *curiously* r. *copiously.* p. 191. r. *Window,* Plate 10, Fig. 7. l. 4. r. *an Angle, with a perpendicular to the Paper.* p. 193. l. 1. f. *Hooks* r. *Hoops.* l. 16. f. *thirty Pound* r. *an hundred and thirty Pounds.* p. 197. l. 21. f. *a* r. *the.* p. 198. l. 3. after *Orbit* r. *it.*

SYSTEM
OF
Experimental PHILOSOPHY,

PROV'D BY
MECHANICKS.

ATURAL *Philosophy* is that Science which gives the Reasons and Causes of the Effects and Changes which naturally happen in Bodies.

And that we may not be deceived by false Notions which we have embraced without Examining, or that we have received upon the Authority

rity of others; we ought to call in Question all such things as have an Appearance of Falshood, that by a new Examen we may be led to the Truth.

This Examen is to be made by Suppositions, which we may rely upon, when they agree with Experiments; but if only one Experiment is contrary to any Supposition, that Supposition must be rejected, and a new one made, till we find that it agree with all other Experiments. Therefore, we must not go about to define a Cause, unless we know its Effects; or lay down a general Proposition, if we doubt of any of the Particulars it comprehends, lest we run into Errors and take things for granted, which have been found contrary to Experiments and Mathematical Demonstrations. An Instance of this may be given in what has formerly been said about Heat and Cold, *viz*. That Heat unites homogeneous Bodies, and separates heterogeneous Bodies; and that Cold unites heterogeneous Bodies, and separates homogeneous; all which we find to be false in several Instances.

1. Mix and Melt *Gold* and *Silver* together, and the Fire will not separate them; neither will
it

it separate two Parts of *Brass* mixed with one of *Copper*.

2. It rather unites, than separates such heterogeneous Bodies as have an aptness to Coalition; as in making *Plaisters* and *Ointments*, &c. and in uniting *Salt-Petre* and *Ashes*, into so durable a Body as *Glass*.

Fire only dislocates the Parts of Bodies, and subdivides them into minute Particles, without respect to their being Homogeneous or Heterogeneous; which is evident in boiling *Water*, or other Liquors, whose Steams condense to the same Substances again. And in *Distillation*, where all the Parts are in a Confusion upon the slackening of the Heat, or the Parts receding from it when driven into the Receiver, they take Place according to their *Specifick Gravities*. Such Parts also, as are most easily Separated, are ever carried first off as in the Distillation of Man's *Blood*; first *Water*, then *Spirits* and *Salt*, then *Oil*. The *Earth* and *Alkali* remain together, because of an equal Degree of Fixedness, tho' Heterogeneous. Cold does not always unite heterogeneous Bodies, but separates 'em; as in the *Urine* of healthful People it causes a Sediment, which is again dispersed,

sed, and made to disappear by Heat. And by Frost, the Strength of *Wine* is separated, and unfrozen in the middle of the Vessel. *Straw, Dust, Wood,* &c. are no farther united in *Ice,* than as they are fettered up in the frozen *Water.*

By *Elements,* the *Philosophers* meant most *Simple Bodies,* of which they said, all the Bodies we see, are made, and which may be extracted from all Bodies. But they have been mistaken in constituting their *Elements,* because they did not so much explain the Nature of things, as what Senses those things excite in us.

They that considered things as they affect the Sight, made only two *Elements*; the *Lucid* and *Opaque*; tho' they gave but a blind Account of *Light* and *Colours.*

The four *Elements* that have obtained so long, only expressed the several ways that our Touch is affected; for those that established them, considering *Heat* and *Cold, Moisture* and *Dryness,* suppos'd 'em the Properties and primary Qualities of all Bodies, and accordingly constituted four *Elements.*

The

The *Earth*,		*Cold* and *Dry*,
The *Water*,	they supposed	*Cold* and *Moist*,
The *Air*,		*Hot* and *Moist*,
The *Fire*.		*Hot* and *Dry*.

To illustrate this Doctrine, and prove that these are in, and may be extracted from Bodies; they used to burn a piece of *Green-wood*, and call the *Coals* and *Flame*, *Fire*; the *Sweat*, *Water*; the *Smoak*, *Air*; and the *Ashes*, *Earth*.

But these cannot be *Elements* according to their Definitions, for they are not Simple and Unchangeable, but may be altered and produced *de novo*; the *Smoak*, which they call'd *Air*, may be condensed into a Liquor; the *Fire* is only *subtile Matter* in a rapid Motion.

The *Moisture* will produce *Caput mortuum*, and *Oils*. The *Ashes*, which they call *Earth*, will make *Glass*.

Besides, several things are not reducible into four heterogeneous Bodies, as *Gold*, *Silver*, *Diamonds*, common *Glass*, *Venetian Talk*. Tho' They and the *Chymists* have often endeavour'd it, and if they could do it, yet they
could

could not prove their *Elements* to be unmixed, becauſe Experiments ſhew the contrary. The *Chymiſts* Principles are *Salt, Sulphur*, and *Mercury*, which they call their *Elements*, but as erroneouſly; for theſe cannot be had from *Glaſs, Gold, Diamonds, Sand*, &c. or may be deſtroyed and produced *de novo*.

Mr. *Boyle* affirms, that *Quick-ſilver* has been turned into *Water*, and *Sulphur* altered; and that the *Mercuries, Sulphurs*, and *Salts* of the *Chymiſts*, are not *Similar Bodies*; whereas, to be *Elements*, each ought not to differ from thoſe of the ſame Name, more than Drops of *Water* do from one another. Others add to theſe three Principles, *Caput mortuum* and *Phlegm*; that is, *Water* and *Earth*; but theſe five are produceable even from *Water* alone; and Art can of two *Elements* compound a Body, as durable as any in the World, *viz. Glaſs* made of *Aſhes*, that hath only *Salt* and *Earth*.

The Doctrine of *Acids* and *Alcali*'s, is as faulty as the foregoing; for none of theſe Hypotheſes can account for Firmneſs and Fluidity, the *Phenomena* of the *Load-ſtone*, the Formation of a *Fœtus*, *Sounds*, and a thouſand other things that fall under the Notice of a *Philoſopher*. And

And as long as the *Chymists*, or any other *Philosophers* endeavour to explain things by a Number of mixed Ingredients in a State of Rest, they will be deficient; since the greatest Part of the Affections of Matter, and consequently the Phænomena of Nature, seems to depend on the Motion and Contrivance of the small Parts of Bodies.

That *Philosophy* therefore is the most reasonable, which teaches,

1. That the Matter of Natural Bodies is the same; namely, a Substance extended, divisible, and impenetrable.

2. That since there can be no Change in Matter, if all its Parts were at Rest among themselves; to distinguish the general Matter of the Universe, into a Variety of natural Bodies, it must have Motion, in some or all of its Parts, which must be variously determined. And tho' it is manifest to Sense, that there is a local Motion in Matter; yet Motion is not included in the Nature of Matter, Cœval with it; Matter being as much Matter when at rest, as when in Motion. And tho' it be wholly disputed, how Matter came by that Motion, by those who acknowledge not an Author of the Universe; yet since a Man is not the worse

worse Naturalist for not being an Atheist; we allow that the Origine of Motion in Matter, as well as of Matter it self, is from G O D.

3. That local Motion is the chief Principle amongst second Causes, and the chief Agent of all that happens in Nature. Bulk, Figure, Rest, Situation, and Texture, being the Effects of Motion, as in a *Watch* or *Clock*; it is Motion therefore that makes all useful.

DesCartes supposes Matter as fixt, let it be pulled into pieces of what Shape any pleases to imagine; we will say Cubick, as most obvious. Then every one of these Parts being turned swiftly round its own Center, and also about another Center common to all the Parts; the Corners must be wore off of several of these Parts, and a fine Dust be made by that Friction. The small Dust is the *Materia Subtilis*, or first *Element*; The Cubes that have been rubbed round into Globules, make the second *Element*, of not so swift a Motion as the first, which is agitated between the Interstices of the Globules; The Cubes that have not lost their Shape, by having their Angles much broken, make the third and unactive Element.

To

To illustrate this Hypothesis, take Cubes of *Clay*, and shake them together in a round Box, till some of them are become pretty near round; the Dust represents the *Materia Subtilis*, the roundest Pieces the *Globuli* of the second *Element*, and such as have not much changed their Shape, the third *Element*.

Tho' this Hypothesis may seem ingenious enough at first, yet if duly weighed it will appear, inconsistent with Experiments, and the Laws of Motion. Take a Dozen or two of Cubes of any bigness, for Example, some of an Inch, some of half an Inch; and having ty'd a Thread to each, and all the Threads to the Center of a round Table, made to turn easily upon a *Pivot*; (*as the Table of Plate* 3. *Fig.* 5.) as soon as you have given the Table a swift Motion round its Center, all the Cubes will recede from the said Center, and stretch the Thread; which shews they cannot grind each other into Globules; since by reason of their centrifugal Force, by which they are whirled round one common Center, they must recede from each other.

If we suppose any ambient Surface to make a Resistance (as the Box does in the Case of the

Cubes

Cubes of *Clay*) then either the Cubes touch one another before the Motion begins, or they do not. If there be a *Plenum* (as *Cartes* believes) the Cubes touching one another in all the Parts of their Surfaces, cannot grind each others Corners off by a particular Motion in each Cube; but must all move together, and become one Body, as before the rude Lump of Matter was supposed distributed into Cubes. If there be any Spaces between the Cubes, there must be a *Vacuum* (which *Cartes* denies) or that Space must be filled with a *subtile* yielding *Matter*; which would be supposing the *Materia Subtilis*, before we suppose it, which is absurd; or denying Matter to be Homogeneous, which is before Supposed.

That Firmness and Fluidity, Heat and Cold, Odours, Savours, Colours, and Sounds, depend upon the Shape, Size, and Motion of the Parts, may appear from two cold Things producing Heat; as Oil of *Tartar per Deliquium*, poured on Oil of *Vitriol*, will cause it to boil and fume, &c.

A solid Body will lose its Smell and Firmness, by the Infusion of one Liquor, and recover both by by the Infusion of another. As *Camphire* will be dissolved, and lose its Scent, by the Infusion of Oil of *Vitriol*; but by pouring on Water, the Smell and Solidity will be restored. *Sal Armoniack* dissolved into *Water*, makes a Mixture colder than each is singly.

Water will be so rarified by means of an *Æolipile*, as to become lighter than Air; and if the Hand be held near the Mouth of the *Æolipile*, the *Water* that strikes on the Hand, will again be condensed, and become as heavy as at first. Several more Experiments prove this Hypothesis. Now if Firmness, Fluidity, Heat and Cold, Smells and Savours, depended only upon a Mixture of Ingredients, as some affirm; then first, two cold Things would continue Cold when mixt. Secondly, A Liquor without Smell would not give Scent to another Liquor. Thirdly, Two Fluids when mixed, would continue Fluid; but the contrary is shewed by several Experiments.

The Extension of Matter, and its Impenetrability, are self-evident; and its Divisibility appears from the Ductility of *Gold*; for an Ounce of *Gold* will guild a large Piece of *Silver*, which when drawn into Wire, will likewise then be all over guilded, tho' the Wire be so small, as to reach above A Hundred and fifty Miles. See an Account of the Ductility of *Gold*, given in square Lines, in *Clarke*'s *Rohault*, Part 1. Chap. 9.

A *Candle* seen by a whole Multitude, shews the Divisibility of Matter to be infinite, because the Rays of Light must enter every Man's Eye; for unless those fine Parts of the Fluid made an Impression upon the *Retina* of the Eye, the *Candle* would not be seen.

Mechanical Principles.

THE Quantity of Motion which we sometimes call the *Momentum*, or sometimes simply Motion, is that Force or Energy by which a Body changes its Place. Therefore we ought to take care lest we should confound Motion and Velocity together; because some People think, one Body to have more Motion than another, when it moves faster, altho' it should be less than the other

other; whereas it may only be said to have more Velocity, Celerity, or Swiftness. But Motion is always estimated from a Consideration of the Quantity of Matter in a Body, and its Velocity together; for the same Force which will throw a Two Pound Weight three Yards (or give it three Degrees of Velocity) will throw a Weight of One Pound six Yards (or give six Degrees of Velocity) and therefore the One Pound Weight, or the Body which has the least Quantity of Matter, cannot be said to have more Motion in it than the Two Pound Weight (or the Body which has twice the Quantity of Matter) tho' it moves as fast again: For if we consider, that when the Force or Motion, which is able to carry one Pound six Yards, is applied to a Two Pound Weight, each Half of the Two Pound Weight has an equal Share of this Motion (now distributed) it will be plain, that the Two Pound Weight ought to be carried but three Yards. The Quantity of Motion may be increased, either by keeping the same Quantity of Matter, and augmenting the Velocity, or by keeping the same Velocity, and increasing the Quantity of Matter, or by increasing both; and therefore the

abso-

absolute Force by which Bodies are moved, is known by the Multiplication of their Celerities into their Matter or Weight.

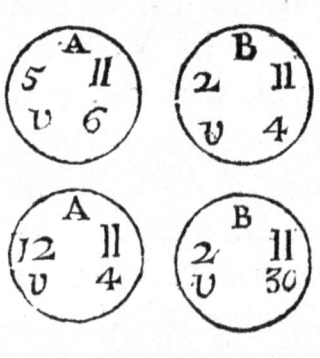

As for Example, in the two Bodies, A and B, let A be five Pounds, and B two Pounds; let the Velocity with which A is moved be six Degrees, and let B have four Degrees of Velocity, then the Degrees of Motion in A will be thirty, and B will have eigth Degrees of *Momentum*, or Motion.

Suppose A to ~~have~~ weigh twelve, and B two Pounds; let A have four Degrees of Velocity, and B thirty, the Quantity of Motion in A will be forty-eight, and in B 60. From hence it follows, that any little Body may have its Motion equal to the Motion of any great Body, *viz*. If the Velocity of the little Body is so much greater than the Velocity of the great Body as the Quantity of Matter in one is greater than the Quantity of Matter in the other, (*i. e*) when both Bodies have their Velocities reciprocally proportionable to their Weight, their *Momenta*, or Quantities of Motion

tion will be equal. As for Example, let A be fifty Pounds, and B two Pounds; let the Velocity of A be 3, and of B 75; now 50 has the same Proportion to 2, as 75 has to 3; and therefore the Quantity of Motion in A, which is 3 times 50, or 150, is equal to the Motion in B, which is twice 75, or 150. If the Velocities of Bodies are equal, their Quantities of Motion will be as their Matter, which is contained in them; and therefore since all Bodies (abstracting from the Resistance of Air) descend equally fast; the Motion which Bodies acquire by their Gravity in descending, will be as their Quantity of Matter. As a *Feather* descends as fast in *vacuo* as a Pound of *Lead*; but suppose the *Lead* 1000 times heavier than the *Feather*, the *Momentum* of the *Lead* will be 1000 times greater; Gravity is the Cause of the Descent of both: Therefore there is 1000 times more Gravity required to make the *Lead* descend, than the *Feather*; so that the *Feather* which has 1000 times less Matter than the *Lead*, may descend with as great Velocity as the Lead, the *Momentum* of the *Lead* being 1000 times greater than it.

And

And consequently, since all Causes are proportional to their Effects, the Gravity of Bodies, which produces their Motion downwards, will likewise be proportional to the Quantities of Matter in Bodies; and therefore the Quantity of Matter in any Body, may be estimated by its Weight; and therefore if an Inch of *Lead* be 6 times heavier than an Inch of *Wood*, there must be 6 times more Matter in the Inch of *Lead*, than in the same bulk of *Wood*; and hence may be drawn a good Argument for a *Vacuum*. For tho' we should grant the Existence of *Materia Subtilis*; yet still the Question will return, how this Matter comes to be so fine, but by having void Spaces?

We must then also suppose the Pores of all Bodies to go in a strait Line, and Horizontally; and they must always be supposed to move in the same strait Direction; otherwise the *Materia Subtilis* would be reflected, and so consequently not fill up all the Pores; sometimes hindering, and sometimes not hindering the Gravity of a Body; so that the same Body would be more or less heavy, as its Pores lay in a horizontal, or contrary Position. The whole Effect of *Mechanical*

nical Engines, is to diminish the Velocity of the Weight to be raised, so that the Quantity of Motion it will have, may be no more than the Quantity of Motion in the Power that raises the Weight.

Suppose a Man can raise by his Strength, without an *Engine*, only ten Pound Weight, with a determinate Degree of Velocity; it's not possible for him with any *Engine* to raise a hundred Pound with the same Velocity; yet by the Application of an *Engine*, a Man can raise a Hundred Pound, with the 10th Part of that Velocity.

Plate 3d. Fig. 1.] Now all that the *Engine* does, is to diminish the Velocity of the *Pondus*, so as to make its Motion no greater than the Motion of the Power raising it, as may be seen in the *Vectis*, which we supposed as a *Mathematical Rigid*, or inflixible Line, only moving round the Point C, which is called the ~~Fulcrum~~, B C, and C A are called the *Brachia*. In the *Statera*, the two *Brachia*, (tho' the one be longer than the other) are equally heavy; and consequently B C keeps in *Equilibrio* C A, which is divided into 10 Lengths, each of which is equal to B C. Let Q be the Weight which is to be found out by hanging any given Weight P upon the *Brachium* C A, and moving it up and down, till it makes an *Equilibrium*, you will find out the Weight Q; for since P in the Distance 5, is *Equiponderate* with Q, it follows that Q is the *Quintuple* of P, as is here Demonstrated.

Now suppose that if the *Brachia* are equal, a Man could only raise ten Pounds; then I say, that if you alter the *Brachia*, and make C A 10 times longer then B C, he can by this *Engine* raise a Hundred Pound; for, because B C, is but the 10th Part of C A, the Space B b will be but the 10th Part of A a, and consequently when B moves, it will have but the 10th Part of the Velocity of A; but by Supposition the Force of A is so great, as to raise by that Velocity a Body of Ten Pounds; therefore it will raise by the 10th Part of that Velocity a Body of a Hundred Pounds. From hence it follows, that the Weight at A will weigh 10 Pounds, placed at B; for, because A a is 10 times greater than B b, the Velocity of One Pound at A, will be 10 times greater than the Velocity of Ten Pounds at B; and therefore their Quantities of Motion will be equal, they being reciprocally proportional to their

their Weight. Since then, the two Bodies have equal *Momenta*, or equal Forces that moved them; these Forces being contrary, or acting contrary, the one to the other, will destroy one anothers Motion, and keep an *Equilibrium*.

A Point in any Body so placed, that all Matter on every Side Gravitates equally, is called the *Center of Gravity* of that Body; the *Center of Gravity* is not always the *Center of Magnitude*, as in the *Statera Romana*, where it's not required that the short *Brachium* should have an equal Quantity of Matter to what the long one has.

The *Center of Motion* is that Point, round which if a Body moves, every Point of it describes Circles, whose Centers are in the *Center of Motion*. The *Center of Gravity* of all Bodies descends as much as it can; and if a Body be suspended by its *Center of Gravity*, it will not retain any given Position; for in that Case the *Center of Gravity* cannot descend. If the *Center of Gravity* be different from the *Center of Motion*, and then if the *Center of Gravity* be put out of the Perpendicular, the Body will turn round till the said *Center of Gravity* be just under the *Center of Motion*, for then it has defcended as much as it can.

Plate 3d. *Fig.* 2d. Let A B be a Beam, whofe *Center of Motion* at m is above the *Center of Gravity* c, if it were turned out of the horizontal Pofition, the *Center of Gravity* muft afcend, Suppofe to k; and therefore if the Body be left to it felf, 'twill turn round, till the *Center of Gravity* comes again to its former Pofition.

In a Balance the *Axis*, and the *Center of Motion* is a little above the *Center of Gravity*; for if it were exactly in it, it would retain any given Pofition; but by being above it, the Beam of the Balance when in *Æquilibrio*, muft fettle it felf in an horizontal Pofition.

The *Center of Motion* may be put below the *Center of Gravity*, but if you move them ever fo little out of an exact Perpendicular, the Scales will not be in an *Equilibrium*; but as foon as you let the Balance hang freely, the *Center of Gravity* will get below the *Center of Motion*.

MECHANICAL POWERS.

DEFINITIONS.

1. *Weight is any Body to be raised, or mov'd.*

2. *A Power is that Force by which a Weight is raised, whether it be a Force that Draws, or Pushes, or Strikes, or a Weight which Gravitates; for a Weight is a Power, in reference to the heavy Body which it may move.*

3. *The Absolute Gravity of a Body, is its Endeavour to descend in a free Medium.*

4. *The Relative Gravity of a Body, is its Endeavour to descend when it touches, something else besides the Parts of the Medium; and that is always less than the Absolute.*

5. *Equilibrium, is, when there is the same Quantity of Motion in the Power, as there is in the Weight; because these Motions being contrary, the one destroys the other.*

6. *The*

6. *The Center of Motion,* Fulcrum, *or first Point, are all the same.*

7. *The Line of Direction of a Power or Weight, is that in which it endeavours to move. In a heavy Body the right Line, by which it endeavours to descend. In a Power, the right Line by which a Power draws or pushes a Weight,* (Plate 1. Fig. 1.) *If C draws A over B, B C is the Line of Direction of the Power, and A D that of the Weight, by which it resists the Traction.*

8. *The Application of a Power to a* Vectis, *or* Leaver, *is the Angle which the Line of Direction of that Power makes with the* Leaver, *as the Angle A B E in* Fig. 2. Plate 1.

9. *The Distance of a Power or Weight is a Line drawn from the fixed Point perpendicular to the Line of Direction, as C F.* Fig. 2. Plate 1.

10. *In all regular and homogeneous Bodies, the* Center of Gravity *is in the* Center of Magnitude.

SUPPOSITIONS.

1. *We must suppose the Earth flat, because the greatest* Engines *are but as a Point, when compared with the Surface of the Earth.*

2. *When heavy Bodies fall freely, they make Lines perpendicular to the Earth, meeting in the Center of the Earth; and those we are to suppose Parallel.*

3. *Tho'* Engines *are imperfect, we must suppose them perfect; that by such a Supposition we may better find out what they'll do, as that Bodies are perfectly hard, smooth and homogeneous. Lines strait, without Weight, Thickness, or Flexibility, and Cords extreamly pliable.*

AXIOMS.

1. *To raise a Weight with an* Engine, *the Velocity of the Power must be increased and that of the Weight lessened.*

2. *The* Center of Gravity *always descends as low as it can.*

3. *A Body can fall no lower than it is, unless its* Center of Gravity *descends.*

4. *If all the Weight of a Body was reduced into its* Center of Gravity, *it would move as before.*

Propo-

Propofition I. Probleme.

How to make a heavy Body feem to rife of it felf.

THE Body muſt be a double Cone of Wood, or any ſolid Matter, as in this Figure. Set two long flat Pieces of Wood on a Table, croſſing each other at one end on another Piece (*Plate* I. *Fig.* 3.) as C C, D, ſo as to raiſe them almoſt as high above the horizontal Plain at the other End, as is the Difference of the Radius at A, and that at B; then lay the Body A B A upon them at D, where they muſt meet in an Angle, and it will roul up to C, if the Diſtance C C be no greater than the Diſtance A A. The Reaſon follows:

When the Body is laid on at D, the *Center of Gravity*, which is in the middle of the Diameter B A, where it's cut by the *Axis* (*Plate* 1. *Fig.* 3.) A A (becauſe the Body is Regular and Homogeneous) is higher than it is when the Body has rouled to C C. Now becauſe the *Center of Gravity* endeavours to fall as low as it can, the Body will roul to C C, where it's lower than it was

before,

before, tho' its Supporters be higher, as will appear by holding a Thread horizontally from D to E; for if the Body touch the Thread when at D, it will be below it when it has rolled to E.

Prop. II. Theoreme.

What is said of the Descent of a heavy Body, is to be understood of its *Center of Gravity*; because unless the *Center of Gravity* can fall, the Body cannot fall, by the foregoing *Prop.* for the Body (*Plate* 1. *Fig.* 5.) A B C D, which stands upon the horizontal Plane F C, cannot fall towards F, where it inclines; because its *Center of Gravity* E would rise, which appears (*Fig.* 5.) by drawing the Arch E F about the Point B. But A B C D will fall, because its *Center of Gravity* can fall, as (*Fig.* 6.) appears by Construction.

SCHOLIUM.

Fig. 4.) Since the first Impulse of an heavy Body downwards, is begun at its *Center of Gravity*, and that the *Center of Gravity* endeavours to get as low as it can; a heavy Body must endeavour to descend in a Line (called the *Line of Direction*, as E G, C O) drawn from its *Center of Gravity* to the Center of the Earth,

Earth, or *Centrum Gravium*, which is the lowest Place; and if it can't move in the Line E G, by reason of the Interposition of a Plain, (so inclined as not to hinder the *Center of Gravity* from descending) 'twill fall obliquely by sliding or rolling, so as to get into the *Line of Direction* C O, as fast as it can.

COROLL. 1.

Hence also will the Body D slide, and the Body F roll upon the inclined Plane A B C (*Fig.* 4.) to get to the Line C O, Parallel to its *Line of Direction* E G.

COROLL. 2.

Fig. 5. and 6.) Hence also will Bodies stand firm upon an horizontal Plain, if their *Line of Direction* falls within their *Basis*. Thus the Body of (*Fig.* 5.) will stand, and that of (6) fall. A Bowl will easily change its Place, because its Base being but one Point (*Plate* 1. *Fig.* 7.) it's easy for the *Line of Direction* E G to fall out of it. This is the Reason also, why it's almost impossible to set a strait Stick or a Needle upright upon a smooth horizontal Plane, because that the

Lines

Lines of Direction E G fall out of their *Bases*. What is said of the *Center of Gravity*, may be also understood of the common *Center of Gravity* of two heavy Bodies, as we shall shew in the Example of the *Balance*.

Of the BALANCE.

Prop. I. Theoreme.

WHEN a *Balance* has its *Brachia* of the same Length and Weight, the Power and the Weight are equal.

Prop. II. Probleme.

To make an *Equilibrium* with an horizontal *Balance*, (*Fig.* 8.) Let the Weight D be to the Power E as the Distance C B of the Power to the Distance A C of the Weight; and so *vice versa*. Thus will the *Center of Gravity* be brought under the *Center of Motion*.

Prop. III. *Theorem.*

By increasing the Velocity of the Power, the Velocity of the Weight is lessened, as has been shewed in the *Statera Romana*.

Prop. IV. *Probleme.*

Knowing the Weight of two heavy Bodies applied to the Ends of a Balance *of known Length, to find upon that* Balance *the common* Center of Motion.

Let A B the *Balance* be twenty-four Inches long, the Weight D twelve Ounces, E six Ounces. To find the fixed Point whence the *Balance* being suspended, the Weight will hang in *Æquilibrio*. Find a 4th proportional to 18 . 6 :: 24: which will be eight Inches for A C: that is, as 18 (the Sum of the two Weights) is to 6 the least Weight, so is twenty-four Inches (the whole Length of the *Balance*,) to eight Inches or A C the Distance of the fixed Point from that End of the *Balance* which has the biggest Weight.

Tho' this is true in the Theory, yet it won't hold in the Practice because (*Plate* I. *Fig.* 9.) the *Ba-*
lance

lance A B, which we have supposed without Weight, can't be really so; because the two *Brachia* are not of the same Weight. Hang the Weight F = to D + E at C, (which by *Axiom 3.*) won't alter the Effect of the two Weights D E. Then hang at I the *Center of Gravity* of the *Balance*, the Weight G = to the *Balance's* Weight; then considering C I as a *Balance* laden with its two Weights, at its Ends C I, find out O the common *Center of Gravity*, as taught, *viz.* F + G : G : : C I : C O.

Prop. V. Prob.

Knowing the Length and Weight of a Balance, *which has at one of its Ends, a Body of known Weight; to find the fixed Point, about which the Balance and Weight of the Body shall remain in* Æquilibrio.

Length of the *Balance*	12 Inches,
Weight of the *Ball*:	16 oz.
Weight of D	8 oz.
Sum of the Weights	24 oz.
Half Length of the *Balance*	6 Inches.

find

find a 4th proportional to 24 : 16 :: 6 : which will be four Inches for A C; that is as the Weight of the Body together with the Weight of the *Balance*; so is half the Length of the *Balance* to A C, the Distance from the Weight of the Body to the fixed Point.

Prop. VI. Prob.

How to make a deceitful Balance, *which being empty and also laden with unequal Weights, shall remain in Æquilibrio.*

Fig. 11.) Let the Length A C be to B C as the Weight of the Scale E, to that of the Scale D. The *Æquilibrium* will be kept if the Scales are laden with Weights, that have the same *ratio* to one another, as 11 to 12; but the Fraud will be detected by changing the Place of the Weights.

Of the LEAVER.

Prop. I. Theoreme.

THE *Leaver* is reducible to the *Balance*; the Weight an animate Power being the same as the different Weights in the *Balance*, and the fixed Point the same as the *Center of Motion*.

Prop. II.

The three first Propositions of the *Balance* are true concerning the *Leaver*. (*Fig.* 12, 13, 14, 15.) C is the *Fulcrum*, or fixed Point; E the Power applied at B and D, the Weight applied at A.

Fig. 12. Is a *Leaver* of the first Kind, as are also *Sciffars, Pinchers, Snuffers,* &c. This *Leaver* has the Power at one End, the Weight at the other, and *Fulcrum* in the Middle.

Fig. 13. Is a *Leaver* of the second Kind, as are also the *Oars* and *Rudders* of a *Boat*, cutting *Knives* fixed at one End, and *Doors* moving on Hinges.

Hinges. These *Leavers* have the Weight in the Middle, the Power at one End, and the *Fulcrum* at the other.

Fig. 14. Is a *Leaver* of the third Kind, as are also *Ladders* taken up by the Middle to be reared against a *Wall.* This *Leaver* has the Power in the Middle, the Weight at one End, and the *Fulcrum* at the other.

Fig. 15. Is a bended *Leaver* of the fourth Kind; but it may as well be reckoned a *Leaver* of the first Kind, because its *Fulcrum* is between the Power and the Weight; when you draw a *Nail* with an *Hammer* it becomes a bended *Leaver*.

Fig. 12 *and* 15.) In a *Leaver* of the first or fourth Kind, the Weight and the Power may be equal, as it must happen when A C is equal to B C. The Power may be greater than the Weight, as when B C is greater than A C, or the Weight greater than the Power, as when A C is greater than B C.

Fig. 13.) In a *Leaver* of the second Kind, the Weight must be always greater than the Power, because its Distance from the *Fulcrum* will be always less than the Power's Distance; for wherever the Weight D is applied; A C will be a Part of B C,

and

[33]

and therefore muſt always be leſs than its whole B C.

Fig. 14. In a *Leaver* of the third Kind, the Power muſt always be greater than the Weight, becauſe C E the Diſtance of the Power will always be leſs than A C, of which it can be but a Part.

N. B. *In all theſe Caſes an Æquilibrium is ſuppoſed.*

Prop. III. *Theoreme.*

A Power which puſhes or draws a *Leaver* at right Angles, has greater Effect then at oblique Angles.

DEMONSTRATION.

Fig. 16. Since the Force of a Power depends upon its Diſtance from the fixt Point, and ſince (by *Def.* 9.) the Diſtance of the Power is a Line drawn perpendicular to the Line of Direction; it is plain by Conſtruction, that C B the Diſtance of the Power applied at right Angles, is greater than C F the Diſtance of it applied at obtuſe, or C K the Diſtance of it applied at acute Angles, and drawing towards I.

F   For

[34]

For since (by 15 *Def:* 1. *El: Eucl:*) C F = C L = C K, and C L being Part of C B, (the Diſtance of the Power drawing at G, and applied at right Angles) is leſs than C B (by *Ax.* 9. 1 *El.*) Likewiſe C F and C K muſt be leſs than C B: Therefore a Power applied at right Angles, has a greater Effect than if applied at oblique Angles K E G.

N. B. *C F is the Diſtance of the Power E, applied at B, and drawing at obtuſe Angles, as the Angle C B E and C K is the Diſtance of a Power ſtill applied at B, and drawing in the Line I K at the acute Angle C B I.*

Prop. IV. Theoreme.

Plate 2*d. Fig.* 1.) If a Power, whoſe Line of Direction is perpendicular to a *Leaver* parallel to the Horizon bears up, by means of that *Leaver*, a Weight whoſe Center of Gravity is above the *Leaver*, it muſt be greater to bear it up, when the *Leaver* is horizontal, than when it is inclined, and the Weight raiſed ; and greater yet when the Weight is lower, the Line of Direction of the Power always remaining perpendicular to the Horizon ;

rizon. The Reason of this is, because the Body does not hang freely from the *Leaver,* to which it is fixed; for if it did, the Distance of the Weight would decrease in the same proportion as the Distance of the Power does, when the *Leaver* is moved out of its horizontal Position: That is, when the *Leaver* I B (where I C is the Distance of the Weight, and C B the Distance of the Power) is moved into the Position O D, and the Distance of the Power at D becomes C N (by *Def.* 9.) the Distance of the Weight would become C *h*, if the Weight was to hang freely from E; but since the Body E O M is fixed to the *Leaver,* it endeavours to descend in the Line of Direction O L, drawn perpendicularly downwards from the Center of Gravity O, which causes the Distance of the Weight to be only L C instead of *h* C; and therefore the Body's Gravity decreasing in greater Proportion than the Force of the Power, (which is a Weight that hangs freely) the Body O requires a lesser Power to bear it up when it is fixed upon an inclined *Leaver* above the Horizon, than when that *Leaver* is parallel to the Horizon. Likewise in the *Leaver* A K, if the Body O, or the Weight was to hang freely from F, its Distance would be t C decreased in the same Proportion as C Q the Distance of the Power; but since by reason of the Body's being fixed above the *Leaver*, the Line of Direction produced is K O g and its Distance; g C its Gravity must be greater, when by the Inclination of the *Leaver* it is below the Horizon Q.

Plate 2d. *Fig.* 2d.) The *inverse Prop.* is true of the Center of Gravity of the Body below the *Leaver*.

Since the Demonstration of this *Theor.* is the same as the other, a Sight of the Figure is sufficient; where you may observe that in the *Leaver* A E the Distance of the Weight is M C, whereas it would be n C if the Body should hang freely; and in the *Leaver* D G the Distance of the Weight is C n, whereas it would be C M if the Body should freely hang.

If two carry a Weight upon, or hanging from the Middle of a *Leaver*, he carries most who is nearest to the the Weight. (*Vide* 3d *and* 4th *Fig.*)

Of the *Leaver* or *Balance*, is meant what *Archimedes* said of his lifting up the whole Earth if he had a Place to fix his Instrument; and it was by these Powers that he is said to have lifted the *Roman* Ships.

Of the PULLEY.

Prop. I. Theoreme.

Plate 2. Fig. 7.) WHEN a Power by several *Pullies* draws up a Weight, the upper *Pullies* are *Leavers* of the first Kind, and the lower *Pullies Leavers* of the second Kind; for in C E and B H, the Powers are applied at E and H, the Weight at C and B, and the *Fulcra* are in the Middle O; but in I K and F G, the Powers are applied at I F, the Weights at O and K G are the *Fulcra*.

Prop. II. Theoreme.

Plate 2. Fig. 5.) An upper *Pulley* adds no Force to the Power, because it is a *Leaver* of the first Kind, with its *Fulcrum* just in the Middle; and in such a Case the Velocity of the Weight is not diminished and consequently that of the Power not increased.

Prop. III.   *Theoreme.*

Fig. 6.) A lower *Pulley* takes off half the Velocity of the Weight, and so doubles the Force of the Power; because whilst 10 moves one Foot, 5 moves two Foot.

Prop. IV.   *Theoreme.*

Fig. 7.) As one is to the Number of the Parts of the Rope applied to the lower *Pullies*, so is the Power to the Weight. *Ex. Gr.* If the Hand can raise but ten Pound without an *Engine*, it will by the Help of the *Pullies*, [*Fig.* 7.] be able to raise forty Pound; or one Pound hanging at A will keep in *Æquilibrio* four Pound hanging at the lowest O, or in the Place of the Body D.

Prop. V.

What a Power by a *Pulley* gets in Strength, it loses in Swiftness, as it does by all other *Engines*.

Of the AXLE in the WHEEL.

Prop. I. Theoreme.

Fig. 8. AS the *Radius* of the *Axis* to the *Radius* of the *Wheel*; so the Power to the Weight: That is, as C D to A B, so is the Power applied at A to the Weight; or rather, as the Circumference of the *Wheel* = Velocity of the Power = is to the Circumference of the *Axis* = Velocity of the Weight =, so is the Weight to the Power.

COROLL.

Plate 2. *Fig.* 10.) This is observed in *Watches*, where the *Radius* of the *Wheel* in the *Fuze* increases, as the Force of the Spring is weakned; that the *Axis* of the *Fuze* may be always turned round with the same Force. When the Spring is Strongest it draws at A when weakest at B.

Prop. II. Theoreme.

An *Axis* in *Peritrochio* is a *Leaver* of the first Kind. A B the *Radius* of the *Wheel* being the Distance

stance of the Power; and C D the *Radius* of the *Axis* being the Distance of the Weight. *Fig.* 8.

By the Multiplication of *Wheels*, an *Hair* may draw up an *Oak* by the Roots.

To this Power are reducible, *Whimbles, Augors, Windlasses, Trepans,* &c.

Of the WEDGE.

Fig. 11. A *Wedge* is the most Simple of *Mechanical Engines*, and is a solid *Triangle*; usually of *Iron*, to slide against the Parts of the Body it cleaves.

To understand the Power of the *Wedge*, one of the two flat Sides which incline to one another, is to be look'd upon as an inclined Plane, and the other as an horizontal Plane; and we must conceive that by the help of this inclined Plane, a Power shall raise a Weight, which without this *Engine* it could not so much as bear up.

Fig. 15.) Let the Triangle D B C, Rectangular at B, represent a *Wedge*, D the Point or Edge of it, B C the Head; and to be more plainly understood,

stood, let D B the Length of the *Wedge* be twice its Height B C, and the *Basis* B D perfectly Smooth, so that being applied to the horizontal Superficies A B, which also I suppose perfectly Smooth, the *Wedge* D B C may slide upon that horizontal Plane A B, without any Difficulty. Then again, let us suppose that the Weight E be hindred from going to A by the Plane H I K perpendicular to the Horizon, which yet does not hinder the *Wedge* from sliding along the horizontal Plane A B, when it shall be drawn or pushed from B towards E, by a Power whose Line of Direction is parallel to the Horizon. If then the Power pushes the *Wedge* D B C regularly from B towards A, in causing it to slide upon the horizontal Plane A B, it will cause the Weight E to rise up by so regular a Motion, that its Center of Gravity E will never go out of the Line E F perpendicular to the Horizon; so that when the Point B shall come to D, the Point C to F, and the Point D to G, (that is, when the *Wedge* D B C shall be in the Position G D F) the Weight E by the Resistance of the Plane A I K shall have been forced to rise by the inclined Plane C D, or F G, which will have pushed it upwards

upwards towards F; so that it will have risen the whole Length of the Line D F, when the Power shall have moved the Length of the Line B D or G D, which is twice D F by the *Supposition*.

Since then in this *Supposition* the Power has double the Velocity of the Weight, it ought to have double the Force of the Weight; therefore it needs not be more than half the relative Weight of that *Pondus* upon the inclined Plane C D to be able to bear it there; according to that general Law of *Mechanicks* which we have taken Notice of in the foregoing *Engines* (*viz.*) that the Power increases proportionally as its Velocity increases: Whence we may easily conclude, that when a Power whose Line of Direction is parallel to the Horizon, sustains a Weight by the Means of a *Wedge*, whose *Basis* is also parallel to the Horizon, that Power is to the Weight it bears up : : as the Height of the *Wedge* to its Base.

COROLL.

Hence the sharper the *Wedge* is, the more easily it will enter, because G, the Velocity of the Power [*Fig.* 12. Plate 2*d.*] will be greater in proportion to F, that of the Weight; and when

this

this *Wedge* shall be used to cleave a Body, as A B C D, the more the Planes E F G O which make up this *Wedge*, are inclined to one another, the more easily will the Parts E G slip along the *Wedge*.

N. B. *E F O must be taken for an inclined, and G O for an horizontal Plane, and the Resistance that the Body A B C D makes in its upper Part when it is disunited from its lower, may pass for a Weight, whose Line of Direction is perpendicular to its lower horizontal Part C D.*

This which is true in the Theory, would hold in the Practice if the Plane of the Wedge, and that Plane whereon it slides were perfectly Smooth, and the Weight truly Spherical; but since there cannot be of such a Mathematical Exactness, the Practice won't hold; therefore Percussion *is applied, which is the only effectual Means, because the Parts of the Wedge will stick less when the whole is put into a Tremulous Motion.*

SCHOLIUM.

The Reason why a small *Hammer* with a violent Blow, will not have so much Effect as a small Blow with a *Sledge*, is, that a *Sledge* with a small Force added to its Gravity, will have more Motion downwards, than a little *Hammer* with a swift Blow, because the Motion is in a *ratio* made up of the *Pondus* of the Velocities.

Plate 2. *Fig.* 13.] The *Wedge* may be reducible to the *Leaver*: Thus C D A is as two *Leavers* of the first Kind, whose fixed Points are at B B, or rather as in *Fig.* 14. it represents two *Leavers* of the second Kind, whose *Fulcra* are in the common Point A.

The Weights to be moved at C, and the Powers applied at B.

To this Power are reducible *Nails*, *Bodkins*, *Hatchets*, *Knives*, *Saws*, *Files*, &c. being *Wedges* fastened to *Leavers* of the second Kind.

Of the SCREW.

Plate 2. *Fig.* 17.] THE *Screw* is nothing but a *Wedge* continued round a *Cylinder* in a Spherical Manner; the *Male-Screw* A B is an outside, and the *Female-Screw* C D an inside *Screw*.

To

To shew better how the *Screw* works, suppose the Weight E to move upon the solid Triangle, D C B from E to C, it will be the same thing as if the solid Triangle had moved under it, and forced it up to F, where it must go, because the *vertical* Plane H I K L hinders it from rising in any other Line besides E F. Now, because the Power has moved the whole Length of the Line C D, and the Weight only that of the Line E F, the Lower must be the Weight ∷ as the Length of the Line E F, which is the Velocity of the Weight, is to the Length of the Line D C, which is the Velocity of the Power.

Fig. 16.] To estimate therefore the Force of the *Screw*, we must look upon the Height of the *Cylinder* H I P Q as the Velocity of the Weight, and the Thread H K L M N O P (if its *Helexes* were unwound and laid at full Length) as the Velocities of the Power: Therefore by the Force of a *Screw*, the Gravity of a Weight, or any other Pressure will be lessened as much as the Spiral Line H K L M N O P, is greater than H P or I Q, the perpendicular Height of the *Screw*.

COROLL.

Hence the closer the Thread of the *Screw*, the greater will be its Force, because its Thread will be longer in proportion to its Height, and it will move the flower.

SCHOLIUM.

If long *Leavers* be added to the *Screw*, its Force will be still increased after the manner that was shewed in the Explication of the *Leaver*.

The Advantage of this *Mechanical Faculty* is, that whereas other *Mechanical Engines* cease to act, and the Weight returns when the Power does not continue to act; this sustains the Weight, and retains all the Force that was communicated to it, when the first Mover ceases to act, because the Weight pressing the *Cylinder* along the *Axis*, pushes the Threads of the *Male-Screw* against those of the *Female-Screw*; whereas an *Helical* Motion is requir'd to unscrew so much as is screwed up of the *Instrument*. Now in other *Engines*, a *Pulley*, for Example, or *Leaver*, the Weight will return as soon as the Hand ceases to pull

pull the Rope, or preſs upon the End of the *Leaver*.

Plate 2. *Fig.* 9.] But then there is this Diſadvantage, that a *Screw* is ſcrewed up as far as it can go in a little time, which Inconveniency may yet be remedied in compound *Engines*, if you make it a perpetual *Screw* and apply it to a *Wheel*, as in the 9*th Figure*, where the perpetual *Screw* C D E fixed to the *Cylinder* A B takes the Teeth of the *Wheel* F, and turns it continually the ſame way, till it has by means of its *Axis* drawn up the Weight G, tho' ever ſo diſtant at firſt.

That this Power is reducible to a *Leaver*, appears from its being a *Wedge*, which we have ſhewed to be made up of two *Leavers* of the firſt or ſecond Kind.

Of the Laws of Nature.

THE *Firſt* Law *of* Nature, is, that all Bodies endeavour to preſerve themſelves in the ſame State, either of Motion or Reſt. So that if the Body be at Reſt, it never comes

comes of its own accord to Motion, but must have something to move it; and if it is once in Motion, it endeavours to persist in that Motion, always according to the same Direction in the same strait Line, nor can it be stopt but by a Force equal to the Force of its Motion. This is plain, for Bodies being of an unactive Mass of Matter can acquire no Change or Mutation of their own State; and a Body can no more change its Motion, and come to Rest, than it can change it self from one Figure to another; after the same manner it can never change its Direction, but will always continue to go forwards in the same strait Line. But whatever Change is made in a Body, must be by some extrinsical Agent; and if a Body ever changes its Direction, there must be some external Agent to make that Change of Direction, and if it were left to it self, it would always move uniformly forward in the same strait Line: If a Body move in any *Medium*, it must necessarily thrust away Parts of the *Medium* that are in its way; and therefore since whatever Motion it communicates to them, it must lose it self. A Body that moves in the Air must continually lose of its Motion; whereas if there was no Gravity,

nor

nor any Air, a Stone once thrown up would go on in *infinitum*, without lofing its Motion. The Air then is the only Caufe why Bodies lofe of their Motions when thrown up, and Gravity is the only Caufe which brings them to the Earth.

In the Heavens where the *Æther* is exceeding thin, and next degree to nothing, the *Planets* preferve their Motions without the leaft fenfible Diminution: From hence we know the way how Motion is communicated to Bodies; for when a Man holds a Stone in his Hand, the Stone participates of the Motion of his Hand, becaufe being in it, is moved with the fame Velocity as the Hand is: Now by this *Law of Nature*, a Body once put in Motion, will always endeavour to go forward according to the fame Direction. And therefore, when the Man draws back his Hand without the Stone it having once had a Motion forward, will always endeavour to continue in it. Becaufe all Bodies affect to move in a ftrait Line, there muft necefsarily be fome Force to make them move in a crooked. This Force may be either a *String*, by which they are tied to the *Center* of their Motion, or by fome other *Centripetal* Force, fuch as *Gravity*, *ty*, which continually preffes them towards the *Center*.

Plate 3. *Fig.* 3.] Suppose a Body put in Motion at A, it will endeavour to move in the fame ftrait Line A B; but the Force of *Gravity* continually preffing it towards the *Center*, that is, from B downwards, or in a Line perpendicular to the Earth, it will move in the *Diagonal* of the *Parallelogram* C if you fill it up.

Plate 3*d*. *Fig.* 6.] When the *Bomb* is by the Force of the *Powder* thrown out of the *Mortar*, it endeavours by the *Firft Law of Nature* to go on in the right Line *c e*; but *Gravity* acting upon it in the Direction *e b*, makes it move in the Line *c b*, *Diagonal* of the *Parallelogram*, contained under the Lines *c e e b*; that is (fuppofing two other Lines to be drawn = and ∥ to the faid Lines *c e e b*) by a Motion compounded of the Force puſhing towards *a* from *c*, and that which puſhes towards *b* from *e*.

Then the *Bomb* would by the *Firft Law of Nature* continue to go on towards *d* in the Line *d g*, being the aforefaid *Diagonal* produced; but *Gravity* acting upon it in the Direction *g f*, makes it by a compounded Motion go on in the

Dia-

Diagonal b f of the new *Parallelogram* contained under a g g f, and so on till it comes to the Point h. Now since the first *Impetus* and *Gravity* does not act alternately, but at the same time all the while the *Bomb* moves, we must suppose the said *Diagonals* (in which the Body moves) to be infinitely small; and then all of them together will make up the *Curve* c b f h, called a *Parabolick* Line, in which all *Projectiles* move.

The swifter a Body moves in a Circle, the stronger is its Endeavour to move in a strait Line, and the more the Thread will be stretched by which it is kept in; the Force by which it stretches the Thread is called *Centrifugal* Force (as is easily seen in *Slings*) and the Force of the Thread which detains it, must be just equal to this *Centrifugal* Force; but if *Gravity* or any other *Centripetal* Force detains the Body in its *Orbit*, the *Centripetal* Force must be just equal to the *Centrifugal*, that the Body may be kept in the same Circle.

If a Body lye upon a Table, and if the Table be moved, at first the Body will not participate of the Motion of the Table, but will seem to go the contrary way; as is plain from a Vessel of Water set upon a Table; but after that Motion is once communicated, if you stop the Table suddenly, the Body lying on it will continue its Motion. If a round Table parallel to the Horizon, be turned round an *Axis*, and a *Bullet* by the Help of a Thread made fast to the *Center*, [*Plate 3d. Fig. 5.*] tho' the Thread be slack at first, yet the Table being turned round, the *Bullet* at C will recede from the *Center* and stretch the Thread as at D; if the Table be stopt on a sudden, yet the *Bullet* will for some time continue its Motion; if the *Bullet* be not put upon the Table, but hang down by the Thread, as in the Posture A B, after the Table is turned round the Thread will not keep its perpendicular Position, but will settle it self in the Position A *b*, the *Centrifugal* Force acting against the Force of *Gravity*, and making the Body recede as far as it can from the Center of Motion.

If a *Glass Tube* be laid or fastned to a Table, in which near the *Center* be put a small *Bullet*, when the Table is turned round we may observe the *Bullet* to recede from the *Center* towards the *Circumference*, and accelerate its Motion.

Besides

Besides this, it will go against the common *Law of Gravity*, and move upwards if the *Tube* be set slanting upwards on the Table, being first fixed to a Piece of Wood, represented in *Fig.* 4. *Plate* 3. and it will stay at the upper End of the *Tube* beyond, as long as the Table is continued in its swift Motion; but when that ceases it is pressed down again by its own *Gravity* to G.

The same is observed when we put *Globules* of *Mercury* or *Water* in the *Tube*. If we fill the *Tube* with Water, and put a piece of *Cork* in the End of it, which is next to the Circumference, we may observe, that after turning round the Table, the *Cork* will go from the Circumference towards the Center; for the Water being more *Dense*, or consisting of a greater Quantity of Matter, than the Piece of *Cork* of the same bulk, it will have a greater *vis Centrifuga*, or a stronger *Conatus recedendi a Centro* than the *Cork* has; and consequently the *Cork* which has much less Force, will be pushed by the Water which has a greater Force towards the Center.

The Second LAW of NATURE, is, that the Motion produced, or the *Mutation* of Motion, is always

always proportional to the Motion impreſt, which generates the Motion. A double Force will produce a double Quantity or *Momentum* of Motion; and a triple Force, a triple, *&c.* and this Motion will always be according to the Direction of the Force which impreſſes it; and if the Body was moved before this new Motion ariſing from this new Force, it will either increaſe its Motion, if it acts according to the ſame Direction, or diminiſh it, if it acts in a contrary Direction; or if it acts obliquely, it alters the Direction, and turns the Body moved another way.

If a Body be once put in Motion by the *Firſt Law*, it ought always to go on with the ſame Velocity, and in the ſame Direction; but if a new Force, equal to the former, act again upon it, according to the ſame Direction its Motion will be encreaſed doubly. If, again, the ſame Force acts, its Motion will be triple of the firſt, *&c.* Thus if A was put in Motion towards B, having once acquired an *Impetus* that way, it would always continue in it; but if we ſhould ſuppoſe that when the Body comes to C, that the ſame Force

Force acted again upon it, it would produce a Motion equal to the former; and both of them put together will be double of the firſt. Again, when the Body comes to D, if the ſame Force ſhould act again upon it, there would ariſe a new Quantity of Motion equal to either of the former, and the whole being put together will be triple of the firſt Motion. If, again, when the Body comes to E, the ſame Force acted upon it, it would again produce more Motion, which would be equal to the firſt; and ſo the whole Motion ariſing from all theſe Actions put together, would be *Quadruple* with the firſt. If this Force thus acting imprinted equal Degrees of Motion at equal Intervals of Time, the Motion produced, and conſequently the Velocity will be as the Times when a heavy Body deſcends; *Gravity* acting upon it at firſt, gives it a Motion downwards: Now if the Body ſhould ceaſe for ever after to be heavy, yet the Body will go on in the ſame Direction, and with the ſame Velocity by the *Firſt Law*; but then in the ſecond Inſtance of Time, the Body is heavy, and *Gravity* continues to act, it will again produce a Motion equal to the former.

Juſt

Just so if the Body should for ever cease to be heavy, yet it would still continue its Course with the two acquired Degrees of Velocity; but then *Gravity* acts the third Instant of Time, after the same manner it did at first, and makes a Motion equal to the first Degree, and therefore the Sum of the whole will be triple with the first. After the same manner the Motion the fourth time will be *Quadruple* of what it was the first Instant, and so the Motions will always increase the Times. This is the Reason why we find Bodies in their descending accelerate their Motions. When Bodies fall, the Spaces through which they descend, are the Squares of the Time they take to fall in, always counting from the beginning thus.

Plate 3d. Fig. 7 and 8.] If in the first Minute of Time a Body falls through a certain Space, at the End of the second Minute it will have descended four Times in that Space; in the End of the third Minute it will have descended nine Times that Space which it did go through in the End of the first. So if the Times be taken in *Arithmetical* Progression of 1, 2, 3, 4, 5, 6, then the Spaces through which the Bodies will have descen-

descended at the End of these Times, will be as 1, 4, 9, 16, 25, &c. If it be asked how far the Body moves in the second Minute? It will have moved just three Spaces; for it had moved thro' one in the first, and so likewise in the third Minute 'twill have moved thro' five; for at the End of the second Minute it had moved thro' four; take four from nine, and there remains five.

The two rectangular Triangles of *Fig.* 7. made up of other rectangular Triangles, represent the Spaces gone thro' in a determinate Time, each single Triangle denoting one Space: As for Example, in the upper *Figure* marked 7, if we suppose a falling Body to set out at the rate of one Mile in one Minute; let the N⁰ 1. and the Perpendicular of the little Triangle at top express the first Time or Minute, and the same N⁰ 1. and the Base of the little Triangle express the Velocity, which always is at the Times; and let the whole Triangle express one Mile that the Body fell the first Minute; then if you consider that the Body having fallen four Times, the Line expressing the Time must be the Perpendicular of the great Triangle, which ⊥ is four times greater than that of the little upper Triangle: Likewise the Line expressing the Velocity must be in the Base of the great Triangle, which Base is four Times greater than the Base of the little Triangle; and the whole Triangle will be the Sum of the Spaces or Miles gone thro' in four Minutes, which will appear by dividing it into little Triangles equal to the first. A Sight of the Figure will easily teach how to know the Miles that the Body has fallen thro' in any Number of Minutes or Times.

If a Body [*Fig.* 10. *Plate* 3.] as A lies upon an inclined Plane, it endeavours to descend Perpendicular, but the Plane hindring it, with part of its Weight it will press upon the Plane, and with the rest it will descend as fast as it can along the Plane; but it will not accelerate its Motion so fast, as if it did all along descend Perpendicularly; thus in falling from B to C, it takes longer time than if it had gone directly from B to D in the ⊥, so that at the Point C it will have as much Velocity in falling from B to C, as it will have at D, in falling from B to D. The less the Plane is inclined to the Horizon, or the nearer it comes to the ⊥, the faster it will accelerate its Motion.

Fig.

Fig. 11.] Thus it will fall sooner from B to G, than from B to C, and sooner from B to E, than from B to F; but in falling from the same Point B to the Points D E F G C, the Degrees of Velocity acquired are all equal, tho' they be acquired in unequal Times. *V. G.* Suppose B C three Times longer than B D, the Body will go from B to D in the third part of the Time that it goes in the Plane of B C from B to C; but the Velocity acquired in the descending from B to D, is the same that is acquired in the descending from B to C, and therefore it will accelerate its Motion in the Line B D three Times faster than in the Line B C.

If a Body in falling from B to D acquire any Degree of Velocity, and with that Velocity be turned upwards, it will just ascend to the same Height from whence it came, and *Gravity* acting upon it will lessen continually its Velocity, in the same proportion it increased before in descending, and after it has come to the Point B it will immediately descend again: After the same manner, if having fallen along B D [*Plate* 3. *Fig.* 12.] it be turned up on the inclining Plane D C with that Velocity which it acquired in descending,

scending, it will just go to the same Height from whence it fell.

Fig. 14.] If a Body B hanging by the String A B down towards E, be moved from B to D, and from thence let fall, it will continually accelerate its Motion till it comes to the Point B or E; and then with all its Force it will go into the Arch B C to the Point C of the same Height with the Point D from which it fell, and then at the Point C it will descend to D, and there it will have the same Velocity as it had before at B, with which it will ascend to D and so make *Vibrations* continually. The Body so hung by a String is called a *Pendulum*. Suppose a Circle, whose Plane is ⊥ to the Horizon in which were drawn several small *Subtenses* B D, B E, B F from the lower-most Point B, [*Plate 3d. Fig. 9th.*] the Body will descend in the same Time along the Line B D, from D to B, or along the Line F B, from F to B.

The Reason is this, tho' the Line F B is longer than the Line B D, yet it is also more ⊥, or less inclined to the Horizon; and consequently the Body will accelerate its Motion faster upon the Line B F, than upon the Line B D; because small

Arches

Arches do not differ much, either in *Declivity* or Length from their *Chords*. *Bodies* will very nearly descend in the same Arches of *Circles*, that they will do in the *Chords* of those Arches; but *Bodies* descend in the same Time thro' all those *Chords*, whether they be greater or lesser; and consequently the *Vibrations* of the same *Pendulum*, whether it run out in a greater Arch, or lesser, are all performed in the same time.

Plate 3. *Fig.* 16.] Let A fall from 8, and B from 4, the Velocity with which A will be moved being so much greater than that of B, they will both meet equally at the Point C; the shorter the Strings are, the quicker are the *Vibrations*; because the String is as the half *Diameter* of the *Circle*; and so the less the String is, the lesser the *Circle* will be; and consequently the less the *Circle* is, the quicker the Body will be moved round it.

The Third LAW of NATURE, is, that Action and Re-action are always Equal and Contrary, *i. e.* the Actions of *Bodies* one upon another, are equal, and the Force imprest is always directed towards contrary Parts; so that the *Mutation of Motions*

[62]

Motions, which thofe Actions produce are equal. This *Law* will be illuftrated by feveral *Examples* : Firft, if the *Body* A moving towards C, meet with B at Reft, whatever *Motion* the *Body* B gets by the Impulfe, fo much precifely will the *Body* A lofe. *V. G.* If the *Body* A have twelve Degrees of *Motion,* and after the Impulfe B have five, then A will have but feven remaining ; and therefore there will be equal *Mutations of Motion* in both, and the Effect will be the fame, as if a Force equivalent to five Degrees of *Motion* acted upon A towards C, contrary to its former *Motion,* and another equal to it acted upon B impelling it towards C; and univerfally when one *Body* hits another, the *Stroke* or *Blow* is equally received in both, and it is always proportionable to the *Motion* loft in *Percutient Bodies.* If an *Horfe* draws a *Stone* which is tied to a String, the Force by which the *Horfe* is pulled back towards the *Stone,* is equal to the Force by which the *Stone* is drawn towards the *Horfe* ; for the Rope being equally ftretched by the fame Power it has to contract it felf, will put equally the *Stone* towards the *Horfe,* and the *Horfe* towards

towards the *Stone*; and therefore the Force of Attraction in the *Horse* and in the *Stone* are both equal; but seeing the Strength of the *Horse* is so great, and assisted by the Ground on which he stands, that he can resist the Attraction of the Rope, he will not in the least yield to the Attraction of the Rope, nor be pulled out of his Place; but the same *Stone* which has so great a Force of Resistance, will be drawn towards the *Horse*. If the *Magnet* or *Load-Stone* attract *Iron*, the *Iron* will likewise equally attract the *Load-Stone*; this may be seen if you hold the *Iron* in a fixed Point, and the *Load-Stone* hang in a *Scale*, or be suspended by a String. The same thing is true in all other Attraction.

Plate 3. Fig. 18.] Suppose two *Boats* A and B floating in the Water, and a Man in one of them. *V. G.* A, by the help of a Rope, pulls the *Boat* B towards him, and that by that Attraction not only the *Boat* B carries to A, but also the *Boat* will be equally drawn to B; so that the Quantity of Motion will be equal *in* both; and if the *Boats* be of the same bigness and weight, they will meet at E the Mid-way between A and B. But suppose B 10 Times greater than A, = then B will

will have 10 Times less Velocity than A, and the *Boats* will meet not at E but at D, so that D G will be 10 Times longer than F G; if B is 1000 Times greater than A, they will meet at the Point D, which will be such, that G D will be 1000 Times greater than D F, and consequently it ought to have 1000 Times less Velocity, so as to make the *Momentum* equal in both. If B be vastly greater than A, its Velocity will be vastly less, and altogether insensible. If a Man in A by the help of a *Pole*, thrust the *Boat* B from him towards H, by that thrusting the *Boat* B forward, the *Boat* A will be thrust backwards towards K.

So that that there will be equal Quantities of Motion in both towards contrary Parts; and therefore if B is 10 Times greater than A, B will move towards H with 10 Times less Velocity than A, which moves the contrary way towards K, so that the Quantities of Motion in both are equal. If B is immensely bigger than A, its Velocity will be less than A's in the same proportion, and consequently its Velocity will be altogether insensible in respect of A's, and may be reputed as none.

Fig.

Fig. 17. *Plate* 3*d.* And therefore if a Man in a *Boat* thrust the Earth or Shore from him, the *Boat* by this thrusting will recede from the Shore; for the Shore may be considered as a prodigious great *Body* in respect of the *Boat*, and consequently its *Velocity* will vanish and be equivalent to nothing. When a *Boat* is rowed with *Oars*, the Water by the Motion of the *Oars* is repulsed back to C, and therefore will re-act upon the *Oars*, and give to the *Boat*, to which they are fixed, a Motion towards D; and it is only upon this Account that the *Boat* advances forwards; for if there was no Re-action, and the Water by being thrust back did not give the *Boat* a Motion forwards, they must stand still, because there would be no Cause for its Motion; but now since the Water re-acts upon the *Oars*, it communicates by its Re-action, as much Motion to the *Boat* forward, as the *Oar* did to the Water backward.

Since *Swimming* is nothing but Rowing with our Hands and Feet, we may easily understand the Reason why by this Motion of our Hands and Feet we advance forwards; for when the Water is thrust backward, it by Re-action will repel the *Swimmer* forward. Likewise when by the Motion of our Hands we thruſt the Water down, it will by Re-action force us upwards.

And the ſame thing is to be applied to the *Flying* of *Birds*, which is nothing elſe but *Swimming* in the Air. The general *Rules* that all *Bodies* obſerve in their Motion, is this: The Sum of their Motions towards the ſame Part, (which is known by taking the Sums when the *Bodies* move the ſame way, and the Difference when they move contraryways) remains the ſame always before and after the mutual *Impulſe*.

BODIES that have no *Elaſticity* after their Congreſs, move together without any Separation towards the ſame Side where was moſt Motion; and becauſe the Sum of their Motions is always the ſame before and after Percuſſion, if we take the Sum and divide it by the Quantity of Matter or Weight of the *Bodies*, the Quotient will give their common *Celerity* with which they will move after their Conjunction. Suppoſe A B equal each, for *Ex.* to a *Body* of five Pounds; and ſuppoſe B at reſt, and A to move towards it with four Degrees of *Velocity*; becauſe B has no Motion, the Sum of their Motions will be four times Five, or Twenty, which being divided by the Sum of their
Weight

Weight (*viz.*) Ten, their Quotient Two will be their common *Velocity* after Conjunction: So that if one *Body* move directly upon another, equal to it which is at rest, after their Conjunction they will go together with half their former *Velocity*. If A and B were equal, and B moved according to the same Direction with A, but with less *Velocity* after their Conjunction, they will both go together with half the Sum of their *Velocities*. Suppose A's *Velocity* Eight, and B's Six after Impulse, the *Velocity* of each will be One; if B moved by a contrary Direction with less Motion than A has, then if the *Bodies* be equal they will move together with half their Difference after meeting; but universally their *Velocities* are determined by taking the Difference of their Motions, which is the Sum of their Motions towards the same Direction, and dividing it by the Sum of the *Bodies*. Suppose A to be ten Pounds and B to be six, let A's *Velocity* be Five, and B's Three, the Difference of their Motion is Thirty-two, which being divided by Sixteen the Sum of the Bodies, the Quotient Two is the common *Velocity* after meeting. If A and B moving contrary Ways, have equal Quantities of Motion, after Concourse they will both rest; for in this the Difference of their Motions being nothing, after meeting they can have no Motion. As for Example, suppose A ten Pounds and B Eight Pounds; let A's *Velocity* be Four and B's Five, in this Case the Motion in each will be Forty, there being no Difference of Motions, the two equal and contrary Forces acting one upon another will destroy one another's Motion; and therefore *Des Cartes*'s *Law of Motion* is false, by which he said, *There was always the same Quantity of Motion preserved in the World.*

If there was no *Elasticity*, the former *Laws* would serve for all *Bodies*; but by Reason there are few *Bodies* but what are *Elastick*, the Rules of common Motion are sometimes very different from these already given; for by the Force of *Elasticity* of Bodies, sometimes they move after *Percussion*, and according to the same Direction, and sometimes they go in contrary Direction.

That we may explain the Cause of *Resilition* and *Separation* of *Bodies*, we may illustrate it by an Example thus. [*Plate 3. Fig. 15.*]. Let A B represent a *Silken-Thread*, or *Cats-Gut*, stretched and strongly extended upon the *Table* by the help of two *Nails*. If the *Thread* taken by the middle Point

Point and moved out of it's Place, so that the Point D comes to C, and the *Thread* lye in the Position A C B, and then left to its self, it will immediately with Force go to restore its self to its former Position. Now by the continually acting of this elastick Force, by which it endeavours to restore it self, it will continually increase its *Velocity* just as heavy *Bodies* do; and when it comes to the Point, it will have a Force to go on forward, equal to that by which it was forced out of its Position, by which Motion it will go on till it comes into the Position A E B, and then it will restore it self again, and perform *Vibrations* just as in a *Pendulum*.

Now let us suppose a *Body*, as D [Plate 3d. Fig. 15.] to run from F upon the *Thread* A B, the *Thread* by this Force will be put out of its Position A B into the Position A E B, where it will quickly stop the Motion of the *Body* D: Now the Motion of the *Body* D being destroyed, the *Thread* by its elastick Force endeavouring to restore it self will return to its former Position, with the same Force by which it was put out of it, and will bring back the *Body* D again with it; and when it comes to the Position A D B, it will have

the

the same Force to go forwards towards F, as it had when it was put out of its Position first. But when it was put out of its Position first, it had all the Force of the *Body* D impressed on it; for all that Force was spent in bending the *Thread*: Therefore it will restore it self with all that Force, and consequently drive the *Body* D backwards by the same with which it came upon it. The *Body* D having then once got an Impulse backwards, equal to what it had at first forwards, will by the *First Law of Nature* always continue in that Motion, and therefore will be reflected with the same *Velocity* it had at first forward; if the *Thread* does not restore it self with the same Force with which it was bended, the *Body* will not be reflected with the *Velocity* equal to what it had at first. [*Plate* 3. *Fig.* 13.] If the *Body* runs sloping upon the *Thread*, the Reflection will be oblique, so that the incident Angle B be equal to the reflected Angle C. If instead of the *Thread* there was placed an *Elastick Body*, and suppose its Surface bended in by the Force of the Stroke from the Position at D B, into the Position A C B, as soon as ever the Force of the Stroke ceases, the Surface A C D by the Force of *Elasticity* will be restored into its former Position;

tion; and by all the Force by which it restores it self, it will act upon the *Body* F and make it move back again. Now if the Body be a perfect *Elastick Body*, it will restore it self with the same Force with which it was compressed, and therefore it will make the *Body* F recede from it with the same *Velocity* with which at first it advanced towards it.

Now that all *Reflecting Bodies*, as *Glass, Ivory, Marble*, &c. are *Elastick*, may be easily concluded from the Sound and Tingling which they give when they are struck; just as in a *Silken* or *Lute-String*, when it is stretched and struck, they produce an *Undulation* in the Air, caused by frequent *Vibrations*, after the same manner, but not so lasting; but it may be more easily proved from the Concourse of *Glass* or *Marble Spheres*: For if you tinge one with any Colour, and let the other fall upon it, the *Percutient Body* will have a greater Portion of its Surface tinged, than that in which it touches; and therefore by the Stroke it must be somewhat flatned, tho' afterwards it restores it self again. *Bodies* that are perfectly *Elastick* recede from one another after Impulse with the same Velocity as before they struck, or they approached one another; or which is the same thing,

their

their relative Velocity before and after their mutual *Percuſſion* abides the ſame. The Reaſon is this: *Bodies* recede from each other only by their Elaſtick Force, by which they reſtore themſelves to their firſt Figure; but that Force is equal to the Force of the Stroke by which the Figures were changed, and the Stroke is always in the Proportion of the Velocity by which they approached one another: And therefore the ſame Force will make them recede from each other with the ſame Force as they before came to each other. If the *Bodies* move towards contrary Directions, the Force of their Stroke is as their relative Velocity, which is equal to the Sum of both their Velocities; but if they go on in the ſame Direction, the Force of the Stroke which is ſtill as the relative Velocity, will be likewiſe as the Difference of their abſolute Velocities; for the relative Velocities are always as the Difference or Sum of their real Velocities, according as Bodies move in contrary or the ſame Directions.

From this Property of perfect *Elaſtick Bodies,* and the univerſal *Law of Motion,* that the Sum of their Motions towards the ſame Direction always remain the ſame, 'tis eaſy to determine the
Velo-

Velocity of each of the *Elastick Bodies* after *Percussion*.

The RULES which they observe, are these following.

1. *If a perfect Elastick Body comes upon another equal to it, and at rest, after Percussion, the Percutient will stand still, and the other will go forward with all the Velocity of the Percutient.*

2. *If two equal Elastick Bodies move according to the same Direction, after Concourse they will change their Velocities one with another, and the Antecedent will have the Velocity of the Consequent, and the Consequent of the Antecedent.*

3. *If two equal Bodies move contrary after meeting, they will both reflect and change their Velocities one with another.*

4. *If a little Elastick Body comes upon a greater which is at rest, the inpingent Body will be reflected, and the other will go forward with a Motion equal to both the Motion of the Inpingent forwards before the Impulse, and its Motion backward after.*

5. *If the greater Body comes upon the lesser, they will both move after the Stroke in the same Direction.*

Those that understand *Algebra*, may easily Calculate the Velocity of all sorts of *Elastick Bodies* after their *Mutual Congress*.

HYDROSTATICKS.

DEFINITIONS.

1. A Fluid *is a Body, whose Parts yield to any Force impressed, and by yielding are easily put in Motion.*

2. *A* Solid *is a Body, whose Parts are so connected, as not to be divided withuot a determinate Force.*

By Solidity, *we don't mean that Property of Bodies, whereby they resist Penetration; but the Coherence of the Parts, by which they endeavour not to be separated.* Monsr. Ozanam's *Definition of a* Fluid *and a* Liquid *are these.* A Fluid *is a Body which is easily passed through, and whose separated Parts join again immediately; as Air, Flame, Water, Oil, ☿, and other Liquors.* A Liquid *is a Fluid, which being in a sufficient Quantity, flows continually*

continually and spreads it self below the Air, till its upper Surface is Level, or in a horizontal Position.

3. Gravity *is that Force which pushes Bodies downwards.*

4. *One Body is said to be Intensely or Specifically heavier than another, when it has more Weight and the same Bulk, or as much Weight and a less Bulk.*

Let *A* be an Inch of Wood, and *B* an Inch of Lead; if *B* weighs Four Ounces and *A* One Ounce, *B* will have Four Times more Specifick Gravity than *A*.

Let *A* be One Ounce of Wood and *D* One Ounce of Lead, if *A* be four Times greater than *D*, then *D* will have four Times the Specifick Gravity of *A*; for there is a reciprocal Proportion between the Bulk and Specifick Gravity of æquiponderous Bodies.

Prop. I.

Both the Superior and Inferior Parts of any heavy Fluid are heavy, and the Superior press the Inferior by their Gravity.

Plate 3. Fig. 19. LET a *Fluid* be put in the Vessel A B C D, I say all its Parts are heavy, and that the Superior Parts A E F D press the Inferior; for since the whole *Fluid* is heavy by the Hypothesis, and the Parts partake of the Nature of the whole, it appears that all the Parts are heavy; wherefore since Gravity is that Force which pushes Bodies downwards, it appears also that this Force is exercised on the inferior Parts of the *Fluid*, which are therefore pressed by the Superior.

COROLL.

From hence it follows, that the Pressure on any Part of a *Fluid* is always according to the Height of the incumbent *Fluid*; for the Superficies E F is pressed by A E F D, and the Superficies G H by A G H D, whose Weights or Pressures are as A G.

EX-

EXPERIMENT.

Take a *Glass* Bubble, and having by Heat expelled some of the Air out of it, immediately Seal it *Hermetically*: When it is cool tye it to a Balance, and add so much Weight to it as will make it sink; then put Weights in the other Scale to keep it from sinking; then break off a Piece of the long Neck of the Bubble, within the Water, so that the Water may run in, and you will find that the Weight in the other Scale will not keep the Balance even; whereas if the Water within the Bubble did not weigh, the whole would still be kept in *Æquilibrio*, because according to that *Supposition*, there is no Addition of Matter that weighs.

Hence it is plain, that *Water* weighs in *Water*.

This *Experiment* refers to *Cor. Prop.* I.

On this Principle are founded all *Water-works* and *Fountains*; according to the Height of their *Reservatories*, so high will the Water rise. *V. G.* If the *Reservatory* be Twenty Foot, the spouted Water will rise Twenty Foot, allowing for the Resistance of Air.

Plate

Plate 3d. Fig. 25.] If you tap a Barrel full of Water at several Places, the highest will spout out the least Way, because its Height from the Surface is the least, and consequently the Pressure is the least; that which is lowest will spout farthest, because farther from the Surface, and therefore the greater Pressure will be upon it. But this must be understood if the Barrel be a sufficient Height above the Plane on which it spouts, as in the *Fig. 25. Plate 3d.* for if the Barrel should lye upon an horizontal Plane, the Liquor which comes out at the Middle of the Vessel would spout farthest; because, tho' the Liquor comes out at Bottom with the greatest Velocity, the Plane would intercept it at a less Distance from the Barrel, than if the Barrel was higher. In such a Case the Liquor spouting from an Hole, as near the Level of the Surface of the Liquor in the Barrel, as the Distance of the lowest Hole from the Level of the Plane on which it is to spout, will fall on the Plane in the same Place as the Liquor that comes out at the lowest Hole.

Plate 3d. Fig. 26.] If the Spout of a Barrel be turned upwards, the Water will rise as high out of it, up to the Height of the Water in the Barrel, *viz.* to A; and as the Water sinks so will the spouted Water without sink too.

Prop. II.

In any *Fluid* [*Fig.* 19. *Plate* 3*d.*] as A B C D, not only the Parts are pressed downwards, but there is also a lateral Pressure, and a Pressure from all Parts.

For when a *Fluid* is pressed from all Sides, it endeavours to recede from that Pressure; from whence that Force of receding will press all circumjacent Bodies, whether *Fluid* or *Hard*. V. G. Let a Drop of Water [*Fig.* 22.] as *a* be pressed by the Finger D upon the Plane B C, it will not only press the Plane B C, but endeavour to recede towards the Parts B and C; and if there be any Body as F, which hinders its Motion, it appears that that Body is pressed with all that Force by which it endeavours to recede towards B. After the same manner in the *Fluid* [*Fig.* 20.] A B C D let any Part be assigned as E, which by the foregoing *Prop.* is prest by the upper Part G, and endeavours to recede towards the Parts F K, therefore

fore it must needs be that it presses F and K with all that Force by which it recedes towards these Parts A B C D.

COROLL.

Hence the lateral Pressure is according to the Height of the incumbent *Fluid*.

SCHOLIUM.

Hence it's easily understood why *Flasks* well stopt, and only full of Air, being let down into the Sea (by some Weight tied to them) are broken, *viz.* by the great Weight of the incumbent Water, which neither the Soundness of the *Flasks*, nor the included Air is able to resist.

EXPERIMENT.

If you immerge a *Glass Tube* in Water, and stop the open End [*Fig.* 24. *Plate* 3*d.*] with your Finger, to hinder the Water from falling out of it again, and immediately take the *Tube* of Water and put it a pretty way into a Vessel of *Oil*, so that the upper-most Surface of the Water may be

be-

below the Surface of the *Oil*, the *Oil* will force the Water up; for the *Oil* at E F being more pressed by the *Columns* of *Oil* G and H, than it is by the incumbent Water at M, will be forced upwards, and it will make the Water at M to ascend, till the *Fluid* in the *Tube* presses as much on the Surface M as the *Oil* at G H does on the Surface E F.

Now because Water is heavier than *Oil*, the Water in the *Tube* will not rise so high as the Surface of the *Oil*, for the Water being heavier, a *Column* of a less Height will press as much on M as the *Columns* G H press on E F.

Hence we see that a lighter *Fluid* may press on one that is heavier.

Prop. III.

Fig. 20. *Plate* 3.] If all the Parts F E K of an homogeneous *Fluid*, as A B C D, which lye under the same horizontal Plane, are equally pressed; from such a Pressure there arises no Motion, for when the Pressure is equal on all the Parts, they all will press each other with an equal Force; wherefore no one Part will yield to another,

ther, but the under *Fluid* powerfully affifted by the Bottom of the Veffel, refifts their Preffure downwards; therefore, from fuch a Preffure there arifes no Motion.

COROLL.

Hence alfo the Parts of an homogeneous *Fluid* are at reft, and not moved by any inteftine Motion; for fince all the Parts equally refift, one Part will not yield to another, and therefore are not moved. Contrary to *Des Cartes*'s Opinion, who held, *that* Fluidity *confifts in a continual and various Motion of the Parts.*

Prop. IV.

Plate 3. Fig. 20.] If any Part as E, of the *Fluid* A B C D is more preffed than the reft, it will drive both the Parts under it, and thofe on every Side (*a latere*) out of their Places. For if the Parts of a *Fluid* eafily yield to any Force impreffed (by *Def.* 1.) it appears that the Parts F G which are next to E, will give place to it preffing with a greater Force, from whence E flows into their Places K E D.

E X-

EXPERIMENT.

Fig. 23. *Plate* 3*d.*] Fill a *Tube* with *Oil*, and immerge the Bottom a little way in a Vessel of *Water*, (the top of the *Tube* being kept stopt with your Finger) so that it stand a good way above the Surface, as at *n*, then the *Water* at *m* being pressed by a high *Column*, will be more strongly pressed by the incumbent *Oil*, than E and F are by the incumbent *Water*; consequently it will (after your Finger is removed from the top of the *Tube*) thrust the *Water* at E and F out of its Place to give the *Oil* liberty to descend, and then you will see the *Oil* come out of the *Tube* in Drops, and then mixing with the *Water* it will ascend and swim on the top.

Prop. V.

Plate 3*d. Fig.* 20.] If the Parts E of the *Fluid* A B C D be less press'd than the rest, the Parts next to it as F G K being more pressed, will thrust it away and possess its room, and the Part E will rise until the Pressure of the Parts next to it be equal to its own Pressure.

For, since the Part E being less pressed, cannot resist the rest pressing stronger, it will yield to them by the 1. *Def.* and that always till it come to such a Place, where the Pressure of the Parts next to it be equal to its own Pressure, where, by the 3*d Prop.* it will rest; but if it be a *Fluid*, and it happen that it rests not under the Superficies, it will spread it self all over the upper Superficies.

COROLL.

Hence if the Parts of a *Fluid* are in *Æquilibrio*, they are all equally pressed under the same horizontal Planes.

EXPERIMENT.

Fig. 24 *Plate* 3.] Take a *Tube* and fill it a little way with *Oil*, and stop it as before, the *Oil* will still remain in the *Tube* (being kept there by the Pressure of the Air) immediately immerge the *Tube* in *Water* (which may be tinged with *Cocheneal* for the better Distinction) a good way below the Surface of the *Oil*, then take off your Finger, and you will immediately see the *Water* thrust up the *Oil* above the Surface. The Reason is this: Suppose the *Oil*
in

in the *Tube* only to reach to *c*, then the Surface of the *Water* at *g* being only pressed with the Column of Oil *c g*, and the Water at S and R being pressed with higher Columns *d* S, *b* R the Parts of the *Fluid* at S and R, being more pressed than the Parts *g*, will thrust *g* out of its place, and make it ascend in the *Tube*, and press upon the Oil which will continually rise, till when it is at *a* the Oil and Water in the *Tube* press as much upon *g*, as the Columns *d* S, *b* R do upon S R. Now, because the Oil is lighter than Water, the Column of Oil which presses as much on the Surface *g*, as a Column of Water would do, must be higher than the Column of Water; and therefore the Oil will rise higher than the Surface of the Water to *a*.

If we try this *Experiment* with Water in Oil, the Water in the Tube will be below the Surface of the Oil, as at G H, so much as it is specifically heavier. Hence we see a higher Fluid may press on one that is heavier.

The same will hold if a Solid press upon the Fluid; nay, even Lead may be made to swim in the following Manner. Take a Cylindrical Glass open at both Ends, and ground at Bottom; then
holding

holding a smooth Weight of Lead close to the ground End of the Glass (with wet or oiled Leather upon the Lead, that no Water may get into the Glass betwixt it and the Lead) plunge the whole in Water till the Depth of the Lead in the Water be about twelve times its Thickness, or something more, and the Water will keep the Lead from sinking; pushing against it by a Force equal to the Excess by which the Water (which is by the Vessel hindered from pressing immediately under the Lead) exceed the weight of the Lead. But if the Vessel be raised till the Lead be but nine or ten times its Thickness below the upper Surface of the Water, the Lead will leave the Glass and sink down, moving as it leaves the Glass with a Force equal to the Excess, by which it exceeds the Water that it keeps out from pressing immediately under the Lead; because a *Pillar of Water* of the Diameter of the Lead ought to be twelve times its Thickness, to be equal to it in Weight. Thus will any *Metal* be made to swim, if they are sunk in the Water something deeper than as many times their Thickness, as they are specifically heavier than Water; always supposing the *Glass* to hinder the Water from coming in to sink above them.

them. As for *Ex. Brass, Copper, Gold, Antimony, Iron,* will swim if plunged above 8, 9, 18, 4, and 7 times their Thickness, because they are about 8, 9, 18, 4, and 7 times specifically heavier than Water.

This Experiment *will serve to illustrate the* 2d *and* 4th Propositions.

Prop. VI.

Plate 3. *Fig.* 21.] Let A B C D be a Vessel of such a Figure, as that its *Basis* C D be greater than its upper Superficies A B. I say that a *Fluid* contained in such a Vessel presses the *Basis* C D as much as a *Prism* or *Cylinder* E G D F, whose *Basis* is C D, and Height E C, equal to the *Basis* and Height of the Vessel A B C D, would press it; for since by the *Coroll.* of the 5th *Proposition* all the Parts of a *Fluid* comprehended under the same horizontal Planes, are equally pressed; it appears that the Parts at C N and D M are pressed as much as the Parts at M N, but the Parts at M N are pressed by the *Prism* or *Cylinder* A B M N, from whence it appears, that the Parts at C N and D M are as much pressed as the *Prism* or *Column*

E

E C N A D M B would press them; wherefore C D is pressed as much as it would be if the *Fluid* E C D F lay upon it.

COROLL.

Hence since *Weight* is as *Pressure*, it manifestly appears that the *Basis* C D sustains the same *Weight*, which it would if pressed by E C D F, which (tho' it seems a Paradox) this *Experiment* confirms.

EXPERIMENT.

Plate 4. *Fig.* 1.] Let A B C D be a *Cylinder* of *Brass*, exactly filled with a moveable *Basis*, so exactly contrived that no *Water* may run out between it and the Side of the *Cylinder*; let *a* be a long *Brass* Tube continued to the top of the *Cylinder*; let a Rope that is tied to one End of the Balance, and runs thro' the Tube, be fixed to the Middle of the *Basis* at *a*, then pouring *Water* in at E, so as to fill the *Cylinder* at A B, see what Weight in the Scale K will be required to move or raise the *Basis a* pressed by a Column of *Water* A B C D. As for *Ex.* Suppose Ten Pounds after this fill the Tube with *Water* up to the top, which

which if it be three Times longer than the *Cylinder*, you will find that there will be need of three Times more Weight to raise the *Basis*, than when it was press'd by only the *Column* of *Water* A B C D; whereas it was then raised by ten Pounds, it will not now be raised by less than forty, which will be the Weight of a *Column* of *Water*, whose *Basis* is equal to the *Basis* G; and whose Height is equal to that of the *Tube* and *Cylinder*, *viz*. G C D H. There are several ways of proving this *Paradox*.

Horse-Hair is reckoned to be a Body that comes nearest the *Specifick Gravity* of *Water*.

Prop. VII.

Plate 4. *Fig*: 2.] If in a Fluid, as A B C D be let down a Body E, having a *Specifick Gravity* equal to that of the Fluid, the Body will be all covered in the Fluid, and will retain any given Position.

For if any Part of it as E should remain above the Superficies of the Fluid, that Part of the Fluid, *viz*. which is under the Body E would have a greater Pressure than the Parts I and K, which are only pressed by the incumbent Fluid. For the immersed Part of the Body E presses H of it self, as much as the Fluid in its room would do; so that the Part which is out of the *Water* added to the Pressure, will force the Part H of the Fluid out of its Place, by the 4*th Prop.* therefore the Body E will descend and be all immersed; and therefore, as in *Fig.* 9*th.* when the Body has an *intense Gravity*, equal with that of the Fluid, both the Parts under the Body, and those under the Fluid in the same horizontal Plane, are equally press'd; so that by the 3*d Prop.* there arises no Motion from such a Pressure: And since the same Reason holds good in every Position of the Body, it is manifest that it retains any one that is given it, K E D.

Prop. VIII.

Plate 4. *Fig.* 9.] If in a Fluid, as A B C D be immersed any Body as E, specifically heavier than the Fluid, the Body will descend to the Bottom, but with a Force equal to the Excess by which the *Gravity* of the Body exceeds the *Gravity* of so much of the Fluid as is equal to it in *Bulk*.

For if the Body and the Fluid were both of the same *Specifick Gravity*, the Body would not descend

descend by the *7th Prop*. But when it is heavier than the Fluid, the Parts H under the Body are pressed stronger than those under the Fuid; wherefore by the Excess of that Pressure, the Parts H will be thrust out of their Places, therefore by the same Excess E will descend K E D.

COROLL. 1.

A Body immersed in a Fluid loses as much of its *Gravity* as is the weight of a Portion of the Fluid, equal to it in Bulk; for *Gravity* is a Force which pushes a Body downward. Now since a Body descends with that Force only, by which it exceeds the *Gravity* of an equal Bulk of the Fluid, it appears that it gravitates in *Water* with this Force alone.

EXPERIMENT.

Weigh a piece of Lead in the Air, suppose twelve Pounds; and afterwards weigh it in the *Water*, and find how much it loses of its weight, suppose 17 Oz. Observe also how high the Lead raises the *Water* when put into it, then take out the Lead and put in 17 Oz. of *Water*, and you will find that the *Water* added will rise as high in the Vessel as the Lead raised it before; and therefore the Weight that a Body loses in the *Water*, is just equal to the Weight of as much *Water* as is equal to the Body in Bulk; what Weight the Body loses the *Water* gets. For *Ex*. Suppose a Vessel of *Water* weigh ten Pounds; if we hang a twelve Pounds Weight in that Vessel by a String, so that it may touch neither Bottom nor Sides, the Vessel of *Water* will weigh ten Pounds and seventeen Ounces, which is just the Weight that the Lead of twelve Pounds loses, and what the Lead loses the Body gains.

COROLL. 2.

Two *Bodies* which are of different *Specifick Gravity*, as *Gold* and *Silver*, *Æquiponderous* in Air, or rather in *vacuo*, being immersed in a Fluid, that which is of the greatest *Specifick Gravity* will preponderate. For since every *Body* immersed in *Water* loses of its *Gravity*, as much as is the *Gravity* of a Portion of the Fluid, equal to it in Bulk; it appears that that which takes up the least room, that is, that which is specifically heavier, loses less of its *Gravity*, and so preponderates.

E X-

EXPERIMENT.

Take a *Crown-Piece* of *Silver*, and a Piece of *Lead* of the same weight; when they are weighed in the Air, afterwards weigh them in the *Water*, and the *Lead* will preponderate.

COR. 3.

Bodies are easier lifted up in *Water* than in *Air*.

COROLL. 4.

Hence the Weight of any *Fluid* is easily found, *viz.* by immersing a *Cubical Foot* of *Lead* into it, and its Difference between its Weight in the *Fluid*, and its Weight in *vacuo*, is the Weight of the *Fluid*.

Prop. IX.

Plate 4. *Fig.* 3.] If in a Fluid as A B C D, the Body specifically lighter than the Fluid be immersed, it will not be covered, only so much of it as is equal to a Portion of the Fluid, which is as heavy as the whole Body.

For

For if the whole should be immersed, it appears that the Parts of the Fluid under it, are less pressed than those under the same horizontal Plane are by the incumbent Fluid; because the Gravity of the Body E is less than the Gravity of an equal Bulk of the Fluid: Therefore by the 5th *Prop.* the Parts under E will rise till they come to such a Place, as where the Pressure of the Fluid A I K D is but equal to the Pressure of E, that is, when the Pressure of the Body E is equal to the Pressure of as much of the Fluid as would be put in the Place of the submersed Part.

COROLL. 1.

Hence since the *Specifick Gravities* of *Bodies* are reciprocally as the Bulks of *Æquiponderous* ones; by the 4th *Prop.* the immersed Part of the Body E will be to the whole, as the *Specifick Gravity* of the Body to the *Specifick Gravity* of the Fluid.

COROLL. 2.

Therefore the Gravity of *Bodies* put in a Fluid is twofold; one True and Absolute, the other Relative and Apparent; by the first Sort of Gravity

vity the Parts of Fluid and of Solid Bodies, gravitate in their Places; therefore the Weights being joined, they compound a Weight of the whole. By *Relative Gravity, Bodies* do not gravitate in their Places, that is, they do not preponderate one another, but hindering each others Endeavour to descend, they remain in their Places, as if they were not heavy; those things which are in the Air and do not preponderate, the common People do not think heavy, but those which do preponderate they esteem heavy, because they are not sustained by the weight of the Air. *Common Weights* are nothing else but the Excess of true Weights, above the weight of the Air; from whence also those things are commonly called light which are less heavy, and by yielding to the preponderant Air mounts upwards; they are comparatively light, not truly so, because they do descend in *vacuo*.

Thus also in *Water Bodies* which descend, or ascend by reason of their greater or less Gravity, are apparently and comparatively heavy or light; and their relative Gravity or Lightness is the Excess or Defect by which their true Weights exceed the Gravity of Water, or are extended by it.

A

A *Kettle* is cold at Bottom when the Water boils, becauſe warm Water being ſpecifically lighter than Cold, the cold Water will deſcend to the Bottom.

COROLL. 3.

The immerſed Parts of unequal *Bodies* of the ſame *Specifick Gravity* in a *Fluid* heavier than themſelves, are to each other as the wholes.

COROLL. 4.

The immerſed Parts of equal *Bodies* having different *Specifick Gravities*, are to each other as their *Specifick Gravities*.

EXPERIMENT.

Take a piece of Wood and weigh it, then ſink it in a Veſſel as far as it will go with its own Gravity, and obſerve how high it riſes the Water in the Veſſel; having taken out the Wood, pour as much Water in the Veſſel as is equal to the weight of the Wood, and this will riſe up to the ſame Surface that the Water did before the Wood was in.

Prop.

Prop. X.

Plate 4. *Fig.* 4 *and* 5.] If the same Body E be immerse in different *Fluids*, heavier than it self, the immersed Part will be reciprocally as the *Specifick Gravities* of the *Fluids*.

For the immersed part of the Body E in the Fluid A B C D is to the whole, (by *Cor.* 1. *Prop.* 8.) as the *Specifick Gravity* of the *Body* to the *Specifick Gravity* of the *Fluid*, and the whole is the immersed part in the Fluid *a* B *c d*, as the *Specifick Gravity* of the *Fluid* to the *Specifick Gravity* of the *Body*; wherefore by 23 of *El.* 5. the immersed Part in A B C D will be to the immersed Part in *a* B *c d*, as the Gravity of the Fluid to *a* B *c d* to the Gravity of the Fluid A B C D K E D.

Hence appears a Method of finding out, whether any Quantity of *Salt* is contained in *Water*, by the Assistance of an *Instrument* made in *Glass*, represented in *Fig.* 20. *Plate* 2*d.* And since *Salt-water* is heavier than *Fresh*; find first how deep the *Instrument* sinks in *Fresh-water*, and if in trying other Water it is less immersed, it's certain that

that *Salt* is contained in it, as being heavier, and by how much the lefs it is immerfed, by fo much the more the Salt is in the Water.

The Excellency of Liquors as *Wine*, for Inftance, is found out by the fame *Inftrument*; for by how much the lighter fuch Liquors are, they are commonly efteemed fo much the better; but their Gravity is found out after the fame manner.

Prop. XI.

To find what Relation the Specifick Gravity *of a* Fluid *and a* Body *given, unmerfed in it, have to each other.*

In the firft place, fuppofe the Body to be fpecifically heavier than the Fluid, and let its Weight be found in *Vacuo*, and then put it in the Fluid: As the Weight of the Body will be to the Excefs (by which the fame *Body* weighed out of the Fluid, exceeds its own Weight in the Fluid) fo the *Specifick Gravity* of the *Body* will be to the *Specifick Gravity* of the Fluid. For the *Specifick Gravity* of *Bodies* equal in Bulk, are as their Weights; but the Weight of a Portion of the Fluid equal in Bulk to the *Body* it felf, by *Cor.* 1. *Prop.* 8. is

that

that Difference of the Weight; therefore these being given, the Relation between the Specifick Gravities of the Body and the Fluid will be given also.

But if the *Body* immersed be specifically lighter than the Fluid, the Specifick Gravity of the Fluid will be to the Specifick Gravity of the *Body*, as the whole *Body* to the immersed Part of it, by *Cor.* 1. *Prop.* 9.

Prop. XII.

Plate 2. *Fig.* 18.] *The Solid Bodies as* A *and* B *being given, to find that Relation their* Specifick Gravities *bear to each other*.

Let the Relation of the Specifick Gravity A to the Specifick Gravity of the Fluid D, be found by the former *Prop.* and let the Relation of the Specifick Gravity of the Fluid D to the Specifick Gravity of the Solid B be found also; from whence by 20. *El.* 5. the Relation of the Specifick Gravity of the Solid A to that of the Solid B will be given.

Prop. XIII.

Plate 4. *Fig.* 6.] If upon the Fluid A B C D, another Fluid as E A D F be poured specifically higher

higher than the former, it will not be immersed in the Fluid, yet it will press its Superficies by its Gravity.

For since the Fluid A B C D is specifically heavier than the Fluid E A D, its Force of tending downwards will not be exceeded by the Force of the Fluid E A D F; wherefore the Fluid E A D F cannot descend below A B C D; yet since it is heavy, it is manifest that it presses the Superficies A D with its Gravity.

COROLL. 1.

Hence the Pressure of any Fluid poured in, supposing it to be Homogeneous, and of the same Density every where, is always according to its Height.

COROLL. 2.

By how much specifically heavier the Fluid is, by so much the greater is its Pressure.

COROLL. 3.

The Superficies of every Fluid is pressed by Air.

Prop.

Prop. XIV.

Plate 4. *Fig.* 7.] If the Superficies of the Fluid A B C D be preſſed by an incumbent Fluid, but the Part G freed from the Preſſure (which may be done by the Aſſiſtance of a *Tube,* as *l m n o,* the Fluid G will riſe above the Superficies A *m* D *n,* and that to ſuch an Height, as that the Superficies *m n* may be preſs'd with as great a Force as A *m* D *n*; that is, it will riſe up to *p q*. For ſince the Parts *p q* of the Fluid are leſs preſſed than the reſt, it will riſe by the 5 *Prop.* and that until *m n* be preſſed with as great a Force as A *m* and D *n* under the ſame horizontal Plane.

COROLL. 1.

Hence the Fluid *m n p q* which aſcends, has as much Gravity as the Quantity *m n r s* of the Fluid E F A D would have of the ſame Height as E A and F D.

COROLL. 2.

Therefore the Specifick Gravity of Fluids are reciprocally to each other as the Bulk of the aſcen-

ascended Fluid as *p m n q* to the Bulk *n m r s*, or when these two *Bodies* have equal *Bases* reciprocally as their Heights.

SCHOLIUM.

Since Air presses the Superficies of all *Fluids* by its Gravity, by *Cor.* 3. *Prop.* 13. If any Part should be free from the Pressure, it is manifest from the foregoing *Prop.* that the *Fluid* will ascend above that Superficies which is not pressed with the Air, until it press the Superficies under it, with as much Force as the rest of the Superficies is pressed by the incumbent Air.

And this *Prop.* is of very great use in *Hydrostaticks*, for by its Assistance all the *Phænomena of Nature* that used to be attributed to the Abhorrence of a *Vacuum* are easily explained. Nay, many things are drawn from it for the necessary Uses of Life, as *Syringes, Pipes,* and other such like *Machines.* But before we treat of these things, it will not be amiss to speak a few Words of the *Torricellian Experiment,* and to shew the Cause of it, from what has been above demonstrated.

EXPERIMENT.

Take a Vessel of *Water*, and immerse a *Tube* (open at both Ends) into it, then pour Oil upon the *Water*, to the Height of four or five Inches, which will raise the *Water* in the *Tube* so high, that it may press as much on the Surface of the *Water* under it, as the Oil does on the rest of the Surface; let the same *Experiment* be tried with ☿ and *Water*. Vide *Prop.* 4. & 5. [*Plate* 2. *Fig.* 19.] Take a Drinking Glass, and turn it so in the *Water*, the Air being turned out; if the Glass be raised perpendicularly, the *Water* will ascend in it above the Surface of the stagnant *Water*, as at B.

The Air does not only gravitate on the Surface of *Fluids*, but also upon all *Solid Bodies*, as may be proved from the Cohesion of two flat Pieces of *Glass* or *Marble* exactly polished and ground together.

That this depends upon the Pressure of the Air is plainly evinced, by trying the *Experiment* in the Recipient of an *Air-Pump*; for after an Exsuction or two of Air the *Marbles* drop asunder.

Another

Another *Argument* for the Pressure of the Air, may be taken from the Recipients sticking to the Plate upon which they are fixed so closely, that after two or three Exsuctions it requires a considerable Weight to pull it away.

Prop. XV.

Plate 4. *Fig.* 8.] To shew the *Torricellian Experiment* and explain the Cause of it; let A D the horizontal *Superficies* of the *Quick-Silver* contained in the Vessel A D be exposed to the Pressure of the internal Air, and the *Tube* P C stopped at P and open at C, be filled with *Quick-Silver*; after this turn it, and immerse its *Orifice* C under the *Superficies* of the *Quick-Silver* contained in the Vessel A D, keeping its *Orifice* C stopped with your Finger, until that it be so immersed that the *Quick-Silver* do not run out by turning the *Tube*; and then unstop it, holding it in that Position. Now *Experiment* makes manifest, that the *Quick-Silver* in the *Tube* C P will not descend below the Height of Twenty-seven or Twenty-eight Inches; and if the length of the *Tube* be less than Twenty-seven or Twenty-eight Inches, the

the *Quick-Silver* will not defcend at all, until its Height *m c* be Twenty-feven or Twenty-eight Inches (there being left within the *Tube* P *m n*, a *Vacuum* of Air and *Quick-Silver*) where it will remain. The Reafon of this *Experiment* appears from the foregoing *Prop*. For fince the *Superficies* of *Quick-Silver* A D, is preffed by the fuperincumbent Air, but its Part C is freed from that Preffure; it muft needs be, that the Height of the *Quick-Silver* in the *Tube* C P be fo great, as that the *Superficies* C fuftain the fame Preffure from the incumbent *Quick-Silver*, as the reft of the *Quick-Silver* does from the incumbent Air.

EXPERIMENT.

If we immerfe the *Tube* thus filled, in *Water* inftead of *Mercury*, the *Mercury* in the *Tube* will defcend, and the *Water* will afcend to the top of the *Tube, per Prop.* 4.

N. B. *If we incline the Tube towards the Horizon, the ☿ will rife higher, and always keep the the fame ⊥ height; for in the inclined Pofition it does not prefs fo much upon the fubjacent ☿ as on the reft, its Gravity acting purely againft the Sides of the Tube.*

P

To

To prove that this descends upon the Pressure of the Air, take a Glass *Tube* four or five Foot long, which has one End (instead of being sealed *Hermetically*) tied over with a piece of *Bladder*; fill it up with *Water*, and immerge it in stagnant *Water*, you will observe the *Water* not to descend at all; but if with a Pin you make an Hole in the *Bladder*, the *Water* will immediately descend quite out of the *Tube*.

COROLL. 1.

Hence a *Cylinder* of ☿ of Twenty-seven or Twenty-eight Inches, gravitates as much as a Column of Air, whose Height reaches to the top of the *Atmosphere*, and whose *Basis* is the same as that of the Column of *Quick-Silver*.

EXPERIMENT.

We may increase the Weight of the Air by sinking the *Barometer* into another *Fluid*; to wit, put it into a long *Cylindrical* Glass, and afterwards pour Water on the Surface of the stagnant *Mercury*, and the ☿ will still rise higher in the *Tube*, according as the Pressure of the Water increases.

About

[107]

About fourteen Inches of Water upon the stagnant *Quick-Silver* will raise that which was in the *Tube* about one Inch, there being Fourteen to One between the Gravity of ☿ and *Water*.

The *Tube* with ☿ being put into a long Receiver, the ☿ will fall down after the Air is pumped out.

The same *Experiment* may be tried with *Water* in the *Tube*, but the *Water* will not subside so fast as the ☿ did. And if in the *Tube* there be left a small *Air-Bubble*, this *Bubble* will expand it self and fill the whole Cavity of the *Tube*, even so much as to depress the Surface of the *Water* in the *Tube*, below the Surface of the stagnant *Water*.

COROLL. 2.

If Air were of the same Density at all Distances from the Earth, its Height could easily be found out; for as the Difference of the Height of the ☿ on the top of a Mountain, is to the Height of the ☿ at the bottom of the Mountain; so is the Height of the Mountain to the Height of the Air.

It is manifest that a *Cylinder* of Water of Thirty-two Foot gravitates as much upon a *Fluid* under it, as the Air does upon the other Parts of it; therefore Water can be sustained at such a Height by the Gravity of the Air.

SCHOLIUM.

I have said that ☿ is sustained at Twenty-seven, or Twenty-eight Inches; for the Gravity of the Air is various and mutable; sometimes ☿ will remain Twenty-seven Inches, sometimes Twenty-eight, and now and then it will ascend to Twenty-nine or Thirty Inches; from whence it must needs be that the Gravity of the Air is changed proportionably to its Height.

By how much the heavier Air is, so much the easier can it sustain Vapours raised by the Heat of the Sun; for Vapours are nothing else but watery Particles rarified by the Heat of the Sun; and therefore the same Particle of Water taking up a greater Space, becomes specifically lighter than Air; from whence of Necessity that Particle must ascend until it come to the Air, whose *Specifick Gravity* is equal to its own, where it must rest; but the Gravity of the Air decreasing, it must

needs

needs be that the Vapours will defcend, which by the Refiftance of the Air in their Motion, are formed into Drops of Water, from whence it cannot but Rain when the Gravity of the Air is leffened; but when its Gravity is increafed the Force is alfo increafed, by which it is able to fuftain the Vapours, and that remaining the Air is clear. Hence it is that fuch a *Tube* filled with ☿, and immerfed within the *Superficies* of ftanding ☿ is ufed to fhew the Gravity of Air and fair Weather which follows from it.

Prop. XVI.

The *Elaftick Force* of Air inclofed in a Veffel of the fame Tenor with the ambient Air, performs as much as the Burthen of the open incumbent Air.

Let there be a *Tube* or a Veffel, having an open *Orifice*, by which there may be a Communication between the internal and external Air; if then the adjacent Parts of external Air, be lefs preffed than thofe which are within the Veffel, thefe will dilate themfelves by the *5th Prop*. until they come to an equal Force; but if the external adjacent Parts (by the Preffure of the incumbent

bent Air) are more preſſed than thoſe within, thoſe that are within will be compreſſed, untill their *Elaſtick Force* is equivalent to the Force preſſing from without.

This appears from Mr. *Boyle*'s *Experiments*.

COROLL. 1.

From this follows the Reaſon why we do not feel the Weight of the *Air*.

COROLL. 2.

From hence alſo we know why we do not feel the Weight of *Water*.

COROLL. 3.

Plate 4. *Fig.* 13.] Let C D be a *Pipe* or curved *Tube* open at both Ends, one of which, as C is immerſed in Water, or any other *Fluid*; the other as E, being longer than C from the *Curve*, hanging without the *Fluid*. If then by Sucking, the Liquor comes to E, until it runs out, it will continue running, altho' you do not ſuck it, till the Liquor in the Veſſel be either all drawn out, or wants a due Height; yet upon this Condition,

that

that the *Orifice* E be lower than the *Superficies* A B of the Liquor in the Veffel; for the *Air* being fuck'd out of the Tube into the Thorax, the *Fluid* under it is forced into the Pipe, by the Preffure of the external incumbent *Air*, by the preceeding *Prop.* therefore the *Fluid* will rife to the top D, until there is an *Æquilibrium* with the Preffure of the external *Air* (fuppofe the Height I G) that is, in ☿ about Twenty-nine Inches, in Water about Thirty-three Foot, and fo in other Liquors proportionably according to their Gravity, and will run out fo foon as it finds a Paffage, becaufe the Water gravitates in the longer Tube; and the Reafon why D E ought to be longer than D C, is, becaufe if it were otherwife, both C and E would be preffed equally by the Atmofphere; if D E fhould be fhorter, the *Fluid* would be carried contrary; but if D be higher than I, the *Fluid* will be forced upwards as far as I, but not farther.

Take

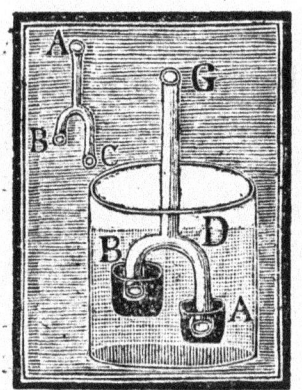
Take a *Tube* of this Shape, open at A B C, and having immersed the Ends B and C into two different small Vessels full of *Water*, put the whole into a Cylindrick Jar of Glass, then pouring in Oil of Turpentine up to D, above the bent Part of the Tube, and the Water will run out of the Vessel A into the Vessel B, which shews that a competent Pressure of a lighter *Fluid* will make Water come over by a *Syphon*, even tho' the Air comes in at G; and this shews plainly that the *Fuga Vacui* has nothing to do in this *Experiment* and others of the like Nature.

EXPERIMENT.

Plate 6. Fig. 4.] Take a Receiver-Tube with the one End longer than the other, and pour *Water* in till it rises in both to the Height A; afterwards put your Finger on the *Orifice* A, and pour in Water at B, till it rise to the top; then put your Finger upon B, and leave the *Orifice* open, and the *Water* will not run out at A; but if you take off your Finger, the Liquor will run out at A
till

till it has subsided in the Leg B down to the Level of the *Orifice* at A.

☿ will rise the same Way, but not to the same Height, since it will rise no higher than in the common *Baroscope*; that is, fourteen times less than *Water*, it being fourteen times heavier. ☿ rises but to Thirty Inches, *Water* to about Thirty-three Foot.

If the *Romans* had known that the Pressure of *Air* could raise *Water* to such an Height, they needed not to have been at the Trouble of Cutting thro' Mountains to make their *Aquaducts* level.

SCHOLIUM.

The ancient *Philosophers* ridiculously explained this by the Abhorrence of a *Vacuum*, in the place of which now deservedly succeeds the *Æquilibrium* of the *Air*. *Galileus* first thought of it, and *Torricellius* maintained and proved it.

COR. 4.

Plate 4. *Fig.* 12.] The same thing holds good of the *Pump*, which is made of a long Piece of Timber cut Cylindrically within, and is immersed in in the *Well*, the upper Part of which ſtanding above the *Superficies* of the Water; which Water is not to be ſuppoſed free from the Preſſure of the Air, but expoſed to it (for otherwiſe the Water will not be thruſt upwards) and at ſome Part of the Hollow of the Pump there is fixed a Piece of Wood acroſs, in the Middle of which there is the Hole D, thro' which this Water aſcends; and over this Hole there is a *Valve* or *Clack* as E, ſo placed acroſs, as to open or ſhut according to its being preſſed from above or below; alſo a *Bucket* as F G, let down from above by the Rod or Handle (ſo fitted to the Sides of the hollow *Cylinder*, as that the *Air* can have no Paſſage between) which alſo hath a Hole in the Middle of its Bottom, and a *Valve* G fitted to it, as hath D E. Things being thus ordered, while by moving the Handle the *Bucket* is drawn up (the *Air* being upon it, and by that means there will be a leſs preſſure of *Air* upon the Water below the *Bucket*) the Water in the *Well* being preſſed by the ambient *Air* will be forced up into the Hollow of the *Pump* through the Hole D (opening the *Valve* E) as far as the Bottom of the *Bucket* (provided it be not higher than I, the top of the

Æqui-

Æquilibrium) as being free from any Preffure from above, and thruft up from below; but on the contrary, by turning the Handle the other way, the *Bucket* is preffed down, and preffes the Water immediately under it, which afcends thro' G D; by this Depreffion E is fhut and G opened, thro' which the Water having got above the *Bucket*, is drawn up with the *Bucket*; when it is drawn back (the *Valve* G being fhut) and finding Paffage flows out at H, then Water rifing again at D, fucceeds as before in the place of the *Bucket* that is drawn up, and fo continually.

Prop. XVII.

Concerning the Elafticity of the Air, and fome Effects depending upon it.

The *Elaftick Force* of the *Air* is that by which a compreffed Quantity of *Air* endeavours to expand it felf into a greater Space; and fince the *Air* at the *Superficies* of the Earth is much preffed by a great Weight of the incumbent *Air*, it muft needs be that it will endeavour to recede from that Preffure every way, and rufh into whatfoever Space it finds free from Preffure, where by its *Elastick Force* it will expand it self equally, and uniformly possess all the given Parts of this Space.

EXPERIMENT.

Let a *Bubble* filled with *Air* of the same Tenor with the outward *Air*, be *Hermetrically* Sealed, then heat it at the Flame of a Lamp, and the *Air* being expanded by Heat will burst the *Bubble*.

If any Elastick *Body* be compressed by a superincumbent Weight, it will endeavour to expand it self equally on all Sides by its Elastick Force; and so equally push the Weight upwards, and the Table by which it is sustained downwards.

Plate 6. Fig. 16.] But if instead of the Weight be put any thing that may resist the retributive Force of the *Body*, then the Elastick *Body* will endeavour to expand it self after the same manner which it did at first, and so will push the Table by which it is sustained with the same Force also as at first; as also the thing which resists it, tho' in vain. *See the Worm-Spring in the Figure.*

By

By how much the more an Elaſtick Body is expanded that reſiſteth any Compreſſion, by ſo much the leſs will its reſiſtive Force be, and ſo on the contrary; and therefore that Force is always equivalent to the Power that compreſſes it. Therefore the Denſity of the Air is always as the Force preſſing it; ſo that ſince the Air within is retained in its Denſity by the Weight of the ſuperincumbent Air, if a double Weight be applyed, it will become twice as thick, and be compreſſed in half the Space: If it be compreſſed with thrice the Force, it will be forced into three times leſs Space; ſo likewiſe if half of the incumbent Air be taken away, the compreſſed Air will expand it ſelf into twice the Space it had whilſt compreſſed, &c.

Hence ſince *Air* contained within the Walls of an Houſe, is of the ſame Denſity with the external *Air* with which it communicates, it will endeavour to relax it ſelf equally with the external *Air*, and will preſs the *Superficies* of *Fluids* with the ſame Force as if thoſe *Fluids* were immediately expoſed to the whole incumbent *Air*; and therefore *Air* within a Houſe will keep ☿ at the ſame Height in the *Torricellian* Tube, as if it was
ex-

exposed to the Weight of the whole incumbent *Air*. Nay, some Part of the *Air* of the same Density with the external *Air* shut up in a Vessel with stagnant ☿, will by its Elastick Force keep the ☿ in the Tube at the same Height as before.

EXPERIMENT.

Plate 2. *Fig.* 19.] Take a Drinking-Glass as A, and immerge it in Water, so that the *Air* may not get out of it; if you sink it all under Water the Cavity will not be filled, the *Air* within hindering the Ascent of the Water; which may be shewn by putting Paper into the Bottom of the Glass, which will not be wet; but if you set the Paper on Fire, the *Air* by Heat being somewhat expelled, the Water will rise a good way in the Glass. Upon this Principle *Diving-Bells* are made, by which divers descend to the Bottom of the Sea and Breath freely under Water; yet the farther the *Bell* is sunk the more the *Air* will be compressed. When it is about Thirty-three Foot under Water, the *Air* will be compressed to half the Space which it was before; this sometimes breaks their Blood-Vessels and makes them Bleed at Mouth Nose and Eyes.

Take a Mortar and bind a Piece of Leather on the Mouth of it, then take a Cupping-Glaſs, and having rarified the Air by Heat, immediately fix it on the Leather; to which it will adhere very ſtrongly, and the Leather will ſwell within the Glaſs, becauſe the Air in the Mortar has more Force than that which is rarified within the Glaſs, and therefore preſſes the Leather outwards. The Glaſs ſticks to the Leather, becauſe the external Air preſſes it down. Upon this Principle Cupping alſo is explained; the internal Air in the Blood rarifies, when the Preſſure of the external Air is taken away and diſtends the Skin, and makes it ſwell in the Glaſs. This is a Proof that there is a great deal of Air in the Blood.

Prop. XVIII.

To ſhew that the Aſcent of Fluids in Tubes after Suction, ariſes from the Preſſure of the Air. (Plate 4. Fig. 14.)

When a Man by the Muſcles of his Breaſt enlarges the Cavity of the Thorax, then the external Air finding room wherein to expand it ſelf, ruſhes in at his Mouth into his Lungs; ſo that if one
Orifice

Orifice of a Cube be in his Mouth, and the other immerſed in Water, then that Part of the *Superficies* of the Water, which is under the Tube, is free from Preſſure ; and ſince the other Parts of the *Superficies* of the Water are preſt by the ſuper-incumbent Weight of the external Air, it muſt needs be (by *Prop.* 5*th*) that the Water will aſcend up the Tube, to wit, that the Parts under the Tube may be equally preſſed by the incumbent Water, as much as the reſt of the *Superficies* of the Water is preſſed by the incumbent Air ; ſo that the Preſſure of the external Air upon the *Superficies* of the reſt of the Water, is the Cauſe that the Water aſcends up the Tube.

EXPERIMENT.

Plate 6. *Fig.* 15.] Take a Glaſs with a narrow Neck but without a Bottom as C, put a *Tube* in its Neck B, and cement them ; then tye a *Lamb's* Bladder A to the End of the *Tube* within the Glaſs, and a large *Ox* Bladder D over the open End of the Glaſs, ſo that the Bladder may be forced inwards and drawn outwards ; when the *Ox* Bladder is forced upwards, you will obſerve all the *Air* within the *Lamb's* Bladder wherein the *Tube* is inſerted

serted will be expelled. If you draw the *Ox* Bladder outwards, the *Air* will rush again into the *Lamb's* Bladder; after this manner Respiration is performed. The *Air* in the Cavity of the Thorax acts on the Lungs just as the *Air* in the *Ox* Bladder does on that of the *Lamb's*. If the open End of the *Tube* be immersed in *Water* and the *Ox* Bladder drawn back, the *Water* will ascend the *Tube* and fill the *Lamb's* Bladder. *Vide Prop.* 19.

Prop. XIX.

Plate 6. *Fig.* 11.] The Ascent of *Water* in a Syringe, arises from the Pressure of the external Air. *Viz.* When the *Tube* of the Syringe is immersed in a Vessel of *Water* at *q*, the *Piston* being brought to R S *is* left void of Air, so that the Gravity of the external Air pressing upon the Superficies *o p*, will make the *Water* ascend in the *Tube* as high as R S, *viz.* that the Part of the Superficies of the stagnant Water at *q* may be pressed by the incumbent *Water* in the Syringe with the same Force as the Superficies *o p* is pressed by the incumbent Air.

R   A

A Description of the Air-Pump which Mr. Boyle made use of.

Shall not give a Description of this Pump as it was when Mr. *Boyle* made use of it; because it may be found in the first Part of Dr. *Harris's Lexicon Technicum*, under the Word *A I R-P U M P*.

Plate 5. *Fig.* 1*st*. Represents the Pump with all its *Apparatus*.

D D is the Handle, which turning with the Nut B B, raises or depresses a Rack A A fastned to the *Embolus* which raises and falls in the Cylinder, that is in the Body of the Pump, and cannot be seen in this Figure, but is represented by the third Figure as it is when taken out of the Frame.

C is a Plate of Iron screwed down with four Screws upon the upper Part of the Pump, with a Notch filed in it for the back Part of the Rack to slide up and down in. It is also represented in *Fig.* 2*d*.

G F I is the Receiver open at both Ends.

G G is a smooth Brass Plate laid on the Receiver with a wet Leather to keep out the external Air.

H is a Brass Collar with Cork and Oiled Leathers, to let the Wire be drawn up and down without admitting the Air.

M N M is the Brass Plate of the *Air-Pump*, on which the Receiver stands, with a wet Leather between the Plate and Receiver.

L L is a Board an Inch and an half thick, supported by the Iron Prop P which is raised at right Angles with the Side of the Pump $a\ b$ to support the Plate and Receiver when the Pump is made use of, otherwise it hangs down by means of the Hinges a and b.

U is a Brass Pipe which lies in a Groove made in the Board, having a Communication with the Cylinder towards T, and with the Plate-Receiver and Mercurial Gage at N.

R is a Cock to let the Air into the exhausted Receiver at pleasure, which will run in from U to N, and so up the little upright Pipe into the Receiver.

O is a Glass Vessel with ☿ in it, to receive the End of the Glass *Tube* or *Gage* N O, which has a graduated Piece of Box to shew how high ☿ rises, and consequently how much the Receiver is exhausted.

S is a Board which supports the Vessel O; *k k* are two Iron Screws to screw the Pump to the Floor of a Room when the *Experiment* requires the Engine to be very steddy. They are also represented in *Fig.* 8.

E is a Cock to let out the *Water*, which must be kept at A B above the Cylinder when you use the Pump.

Fig. 3. Represents a Brass Cylinder Cleft at the Bottom, for the *Piston* represented by *Fig.* 4. to move up and down in. This Cylinder is screwed down to the Stool of the Pump, being let down into the Box under A B; and there is a Cement made of Pitch and Brick-Dust poured hot into the Box about the outside of the Cylinder, which growing hard when cold, keeps it fixed.

T is a Hole to receive the Screw of the Pipe X Y, of *Fig.* 7.

Fig. 4. Represents the Rack A and *Embolus* B B, which makes up the *Piston* of the Pump.

g g is a Brass Plate fixed to the Rack about a quarter of an Inch less in Diameter than the inner Diameter of the Cylinder.

e e f f represent three or four round Pieces of *Sheep*'s Leather oiled very soft, about half an Inch more in Diameter than the Bore of the Cylinder, which being put on immediately below the Plate *g g*, will fold round the said Plate up towards A when the *Piston* is let down into the Cylinder.

c d is a stiff Piece of Shoe-Sole-Leather, whose Diameter is so nearly equal to that of the Cylinder's Bore, that it must but just slip down into the Cylinder without Friction.

B B is a Brass Plate screwed on at the Bottom of the Rack to keep the whole *Embolus* together.

When this *Piston* is let down into the Cylinder below the Hole T, *Fig.* 1. the Air between T and U easily passes upwards by the Side of the *Embolus*, folding the left Leather up round the Plate *g g*, *Fig.* 4. but when you draw it from the Bottom no Air can get down below the *Embolus*, because the Space between the Sides of the Cylinder and the Plate *c d*, is not large enough to let the Air fold downwards; so that the Pressure of the Air and Water (which always lies on the *Embolus*, the more the

soft

soft Leather is pressed to the Sides of the Cylinder, and therefore the Passage downwards round the *Embolus* must be close stopped and keep out the Air, even tho' the Bore of the Cylinder should not be truly round, as it happens in this, which by long use was become a little Oval.

Fig. 7. is a more exact Representation of the Pipe U T of *Fig.* 1.

Y X is that Part which is to screw into the Cylinder, having a square Place at *a* to receive the Key of *Fig.* 5. which serves to turn all the Screws with its End *s*, or its End *r*.

Fig. 7. *c a b* is that Part of the Pipe which lies under the Plate that is screwed on at *z*.

c is to screw on the Part Y at T in *Fig.* 1.

a is a Screw to receive a Gage at the Place marked N in *Fig.* 1. It must have a *Valve* of a wet Bladder at the End of the Screw *b*, to which the Cock R is to be screwed, by applying the Key Q *Fig.* 5. to the square Place near *b*. *Fig.* 1.

Fig. 6. is the Brass Plate a quarter of an Inch thick, which is truly flat, having a Brass Rim round it to keep the Water from spilling when it is made use of in any Experiment.

P

P is a Hole in the Plate with a Screw to receive the little Pipe that stands upright under the Receiver.

N is the Plate with the Bottom upwards, shewing the Screw that fills the Hole *z* of the Pipe of *Fig.* 7. at the Place marked N in *Fig.* 1.

The Receiver is Exhausted in the following manner.

When by means of the Handle or Winch D D the *Embolus* is raised above the Level of the Pipe U T in *Fig.* 1. (that is above the Hole T of the Cylinder in *Fig.* 3.) there is a *Vacuum* in the Cylinder under the *Embolus* and in the Pipe T L; *Fig.* 1. so that the *Valve* at T being no longer pressed, the Air in the Receiver easily lifts it up by its Elasticity, expands it self so as to fill the void Cylinder. Then depressing the *Embolus* the Air comes up out of the Cylinder betwixt its Sides and the *Embolus*, and so comes bubbling out thro' the Water at A B, and raising the *Piston* a second time, the Air in the Receiver (tho' pretty much rarified already) lifts up the *Valve* at T, and runs into the Cylinder with Ease, to fill the void Space under the *Embolus*, and then is expressed out as
be-

before; and so on till the Receiver is quite exhausted, which may be known by the rising of ☿ in the Gage; for when it is got up to the same Height as that at which it stands in the *Barometer*, the Receiver is exhausted; because the Pressure of the Air being wholly taken off from that part of the Surface of ☿ which is directly under the *Tube*, the external Air will press upon the other Part of the Surface of the stagnant ☿, and so raise the ☿ in the *Tube*, till it makes an *Æquilibrium* with the Weight of the *Atmosphere*.

N. B. *Tho' the external Air can come into the Pipe L T, it cannot get into the exhausted Receiver, because the Valve is shut the closer towards N M the more the Air presses upon it, being made only to open towards L.*

Experiments *of the* Air-Pump.

1. LAY your Hand on the Mouth of a small Receiver, and by the Pump draw out the Air, and your Hand will swell within the Receiver; after a few Suctions the Air will press upon your Hand so that you cannot raise it.

2. Tie a Bladder to the Mouth of a Receiver, and extract the Air; then the external Air will depress the Bladder so much, that a Man's Strength will not be able to sustain it.

3. Invert a Receiver, and tie a Weight to the Neck of a Bladder over the Mouth of the Receiver, and hanging on the outside of it; having drawn the Air out of the Receiver, the outward Air will press so on the Bladder, as to thrust it up into the Receiver, and raise the Weight.

4. Take a Piece of Glass and put it on the Mouth of a Receiver, having drawn out the Air, the Weight of the incumbent Air pressing on the Glass will break it. By this *Experiment* we prove that the Air presses every way; for in what Position soever the Glass be, it will still be broken by the incumbent Air

This is also proved by the strong Cohesion of two flat Pieces of Glass or Marble, exactly polished and ground together. As also by a Glass Recipient sticking so close to the Plate, after the Exsuction of the Air, that it requires a considerable Weight to pull it away.

S   5. In

5. In the *Torcellian Experiment*, if the *Tube* with the *Mercury* be put into a long Receiver, the ☿ will fall down at the Exsuction of the Air.

6. The same *Experiment* may be tried with *Water* in the *Tube*; but it is observed that the *Water* will subside so fast as ☿.

7. If in the *Tube* there be left a small Air-Bubble, the Bubble will expand it self and fill the whole Capacity of the *Tube*, even so much as to depress the Surface of the *Water*, under the Surface of the stagnant *Water*.

8. A flavid Bladder, after the Pressure of the external Air is taken off, dilates it self as far as it can.

9. The Expansion of the *Air* in a Bladder, will raise a Weight after the external *Air* is taken away.

10. A Bladder in which Weights are put to sink it under *Water*, will rise with its Weight after the Extraction of the external *Air*.

11. A Piece of Cork, to which is tied just so much Weight as to make it sink all under *Water*, except the upper Surface of it, after the Air is extracted, will rise higher; but when you let in the Air again it will immediately sink towards the Bottom.

12. Fishes

12. Fishes in the *Water* in the Recipient will rise to the top of the *Water* when the Air is drawn out.

13. A Glass Bubble in which is left just so much *Water* as will sink it, after the Extraction of the external Air will rise.

14. If you draw out the Air from a square Glass Bottle, the Weight of the incumbent Air will break it to pieces.

15. If you put such a Bottle so closely stopt, that none of the Air can get out of it into the Receiver; after you have drawn out the external Air, that which is in the Bottle will so dilate it self, as to break the Bottle.

16. If you put two Brass *Hemispheres* together, shutting them one within the other, and only putting a Piece of wet Leather between them; if after this you pump out all the Air by the Help of a *Valve* at the Bottom of one of the *Hemispheres*, the Air cannot return into them; they will stick so closely by reason of the external Air, that it will require a very great Force to pull them asunder.

17. If you put any *Animal* into the Receiver, and pump out the Air, the *Animal* will immediately die.

18. If you take a Glaſs *Bottle* half full of *Water*, having a Glaſs Tube cemented in the Neck of it, one End of which is below the Surface of the *Water*, and the other being above the top of the *Bottle*, has a *Braſs* Top with ſmall Holes in it; if you put this into the Receiver, and pump out the Air, the Air in the *Bottle* will dilate it ſelf ſo as to preſs on the Surface of the *Water*, and raiſe it up in Spouts thro' the Holes of the Tube like a Fountain.

19. If you put a *Bell* ſo raiſed on a wooden Frame, that it may have room to move into a Receiver, and pump the Air out; then if you ſhake the Pump, ſo as to move the *Bell*, you will hardly hear the Sound of it.

This is a Proof that Sounds depend on the *Air*.

20. If you put a Glaſs of warm *Water* into the Receiver, and pump out the *Air*, the *Water* will perfectly ſeem to boil; the Reaſon is this, *viz.* The Elaſtick Force of the *Air* which is in the *Water* being increaſed by Heat, and not being preſſed by any external Air, it endeavours to dilate it ſelf, and by that means makes the Water bubble up; this is the way by which the *Air* may be almoſt all Extracted from the *Water*.

How

How to Condense the AIR, so that you may put what Quantity you please into a Vessel.

Plate 4. Fig. 10. IF you have a *Brass* Vessel half full of *Water*, with a Hole on the top of it, into which you may screw a little *Brass Pipe* at A, with a Cock at B, by which you may let in the *Air*; if on this you screw a Syringe which has at the bottom a *Valve*, by which the *Air* forced into the Pipe may be kept from returning again; and likewise a Curve Tube screwed to it at C, or only a small Hole and a *Valve* at the same Place, if then you draw up the Sucker of the Syringe, the Air will come in thro' the Tube D into the Syringe at C, and the *Valve* will then hinder it from returning. If then you open the Cock at B, and thrust down the Sucker, the Air will likewise descend into the Vessel, and by the *Valve* at the bottom of the Syringe be hindered

from

from returning; by repeating this often, you may put what Quantity of *Air* you please into a Vessel. If then you take off the Syringe, and screw on in the place of it a Pipe with Holes, when you open the Cork, the *Air* pressing hard on the *Water*, will force it up to a great Height, and will spout out in Figures according to the Holes of the Pipe.

Of Barometers, Thermometers, *and* Hydrometers.

IS evident by what has been already proved, that the ☿ within the Tube gravitates as much on the Surface of the stagnant Mercury, as the *Air* does on the rest of its Surface; and that a Column of *Air* reaching to the top of the *Atmosphere*, is of the same Weight with a Column of *Mercury* of the same *Basis*, and of an Height equal to the ☿ in the Tube. Now if the *Air* should grow heavier, and press more on the Surface of the stagnant

nant ☿, then the ☿ in the Tube muſt riſe higher, that it may be equal in Weight to a Column of *Air* of the ſame *Baſis*, reaching to the top of the *Atmoſphere*.

Hence it follows, that the Height of the ☿ in the Tube may be fitly applied to meaſure the Gravity of the *Air*, and on that Account an Inſtrument filled to that Purpoſe is called a B A-ROMETER.

Sometimes ☿ riſes Thirty Inches, ſometimes it ſtands at Twenty-nine, ſometimes at Twenty-eight, ſometimes it will ſink to Twenty-ſeven, but ſeldom under, and of conſequence the Gravity of the *Air* muſt alter proportionably.

Since Gravity is always proportionable to what the Matter weighs, it is impoſſible that the *Air* ſhould change its Gravity, without changing its Quantity of Matter; and therefore ſome have thought this Difference of the *Air's* Gravity to proceed from its being more or leſs over-charged with Vapours; if this were the Caſe, there muſt be as many Vapours in the Air at a time, as are equal to Three Inches of ☿, for ſo much we find the ☿ riſes or falls.

Now

Now ☿ is about Fourteen Times heavier than *Water*, and consequently there must be in the Air at once, as many Vapours as will equal in length a Column of *Water* of Forty-two Inches high, and whose *Basis* is equal to the Surface of the Earth; which is more than falls down in Rain during a whole Year; for a whole Year's Rain does not fill a Vessel above Fourteen or Fifteen Inches high, as is observed in the History of the *Royal Society* at *Paris*.

The Reason then why the Air is heavier at one time than another, arises from their being more Air in that part of the Earth's Surface, where the Air grows heavier, and this proceeds from *Winds*. *V. G.* If the *Wind* (which is nothing but a Stream of Air) should blow over any Place, and the Air thus moved should be kept in that Place by Mountains or Hills; or if two contrary *Winds* should blow on the same Place, the Air would be heaped up in the Middle, and consequently there being more Air, its Gravity will be increased; but if a *Wind* should blow over a Country, the Air which is over that Place will be less in Quantity and consequently lighter. Hence it is plain, that *Winds* are the only Cause of the Air's Gravity.

When

When the Air is heavy, the Sun acting on the Surface of the *Water* raises the Vapours from it; these being raised are specifically lighter than Air, and consequently they must rise higher, till they come to an Air of the same Specifick Gravity with themselves, where they will rest; and a vast Collection of these Vapours from Clouds, so long as the Air continues heavy, the Vapours will be sustained, and the Weather will be Fair. But if the Air turns lighter, the Vapours which were in *Æquilibrio* with it before, will now preponderate, and consequently descend; in their Descent being continually checked by the great Resistance of Air with which they meet, they will be condensed; this Condensation will still grow more and more, till at last they are formed into Drops of Rain.

Hence it follows, that when the ☿ in the Tube is high, then the Weather will be Fair, and when it falls low, the Vapours then not being sufficiently sustained by the Air, must also fall, and the Weather will be rainy, and the Rain more or less according as the *Mercury* rises or falls in the Tube.

Upon this Principle common *Weather-Glasses* are made; but to make the Change of the Air's Gravity more visible, several Instruments have been contrived.

Plate 2. *Fig.* 21.] The *Wheel-Barometer* which consists of a *Recurve* Tube A B C G E filled with ☿, the Gravity of the Air pressing on the Surface E, there swims a *Leaden Ball* tied to a String, at the other End of which there is also tied a Weight, and the String runs on a Pulley at C, to which there is an Hand or Index applied, which moves along with the Pulley; and a large Piece of *Brass* B F G E divided into any Number of equal Parts, marked 1, 2, 3, &c. When the ☿ falls at B it must rise at E, and consequently raise the *Ball* with it, whereupon the Weight at D will descend lower, and draw the String with it; and by this Motion the Pulley being turned, the Hand will shew the least Variation of the Air.

This was invented by Dr. *Hook*; but this Instrument has one Inconvenience which makes it almost useless; for in damp Weather the String to which the Weights are tied, is contracted; and in dry it will grow longer; by this Motion it will move the Hand, when in the mean time the ☿

has

has neither risen nor fallen. A Watch String will do better with an *Iron Ball* instead of a *Leaden* one, which would be eaten up by the ☿.

Plate 6. Fig. 18.] 2. *HUGENS* contrived another Instrument after this manner. A B C D E F is a *Recurve Tube*, so made that the two Parts of it A B and D E have a much greater *Basis* than the rest, the *Tube* being filled with ☿, the Gravity of the Air pressing on the Surface at G, will sustain the ☿ to the Height A B, the Parts A B and D E being of an equal Height; if the ☿ fall an Inch at A B, it will rise as much at D E. Thro' the Orifice M on the Surface D E is poured Oil of *Tartar per Deliquium*, or *Spirits of Wine*, or some other Liquor that will not Freeze, to the Height F. Now when the ☿ rises at D E but an Inch, it will raise the Liquor which is poured into the Tube K I an Inch; and the slender Tube M P being of a much less *Basis* than the Tube K I, it must rise higher in M P. Thus if the *Basis* D E be ten times greater than O P, for one Inch that the Liquor rises in the Tube K I, it will rise ten Inches in the slender Tube M P. If ☿ falls one Inch in the Tube A B, the Liquor will rise ten in M P.

This Sort of *Barometer* has also an Inconvenience, which is, that as the Weather is Hot or Cold, so the Liquor in the Tube M P will dilate or contract it self, and consequently rise or fall; whereas the ☿ continues still the same Height.

3. Since ☿ in a Tube keeps always the same ⊥ Height, however the Tube be inclined; the best Contrivance for a *Barometer* seems to be this. A B C is a Tube (*Plate 6. Fig. 3.*) bended as in the Figure; B C is about Twenty-six Inches long, and A B so inclined that it may be Fifteen, whereas the ⊥ A E would not be above Five, according to the Structure, for every Inch the ☿ rises in the ordinary Tube, it will rise Three in the inclined one A B.

As *BAROMETERS* shew the different Changes of *Air*, as to Gravity and Levity, whence we estimate Fair and Foul-weather; so *Thermometers* are made use of to measure the various Temperature of the *Air*, as to Heat and Cold; to discover which there are several Instruments contrived.

Plate 6. Fig. 13.] 1. The First is almost in the Form of a *Barometer*, only the upper End of the Tube

Tube ends in a large *Glass Ball*. This *Ball* is heated by putting near the Fire, so that the Air in it will be rarified, and somewhat expelled by Heat; then immediately the Neck of the Tube is to be immersed in stagnant Water, which should be tinged with some Colour that it may more easily be perceived. As *Air* in the *Ball* A begins to cool, it being more rare and less compressed than the external *Air*, the Water in the Vessel will be impelled up into the Tube to B, by the Force of the external *Air*, and so compress the *Air* in A as much as the external *Air* is compressed. Now if the *Air* in A be afterwards again more heated, it will endeavour to expand it self, and fill up a greater Space, and so press the Water down; but when it grows cooler it will be contracted into a less Compass, and the Water will again ascend; so that when the Water in the Tube descends, the *Air* is hotter, and when the Water ascends, the *Air* is cooler.

Plate 6. *Fig.* 1.] 2. The second Kind of *THERMOSCOPE* is by a *Recurve Tube*, thro' the Orifice of which at D, the tinged Water is poured, and fills up the Space B C, compressing the *Air* in the Globe A, in which, when

the

the *Air* grows more hot, it expands it self and takes up the greater room by preſſing the *Water* in the Tube upwards to D; and when the *Air* is cooled, it is again condenſed, and the Water falls down; ſo that the riſing of the Water denotes its Heat, and the falling the Coldneſs of the Air, contrary to what is done in the firſt Sort.

Plate 6. *Fig.* 12.] 3. The third Sort is in this Faſhion. Thro' the narrow Neck of a Glaſs *Bottle* filled with Water, is put a long Tube open at both Ends, the lower End of which is immerſed below the Water; after having fixed the Tube with Cement, ſo that there can be no Communication between the external Air and that in the *Phial*, Air is blown ſtrongly thro' the Tube, by which the Air in the *Phial* is compreſſed; and therefore it will preſs the Water up to D; and if the Air always continues in the ſame Tenor as to Heat and Cold, the Water would always continue in the ſame Station; but when the Air in the *Phial* grows hotter, it will endeavour to expand it ſelf, and preſs more ſtrongly on the Surface of the Water, and raiſe it higher in the Tube.

In theſe Sorts of *Thermometers*, and all others which have any Communication with the external Air,

Air, the Liquor will not only be raised or depressed by the Change of Air, as to Heat or Cold; but also to any Alteration as to Gravity or Levity; and consequently the Temperature of the Air as to Heat and Cold may remain, when nevertheless the Height of the Water may be considerably altered.

Plate 6. *Fig.* 5.] 4. This Sort of *THERMOSCOPE* is not liable to the same Inconvenience. It is a long Tube with a Glass Ball at the End of it, which being filled with high and rectified *Spirits of Wine* half up to D, the remaining empty Part C is considerably heated, that the *Air* may be expelled; after this the top of the Tube is to be immediately Sealed *Hermetically*, so that the *Air* may not re-enter the Tube; then the Rarefaction and Condensation of the *Spirits of Wine*, by which it rises or falls in the Tube, according to the Degrees of Heat or Cold, shew the Temperature of the *Air* as to Heat and Cold.

Plate 6. *Fig.* 14.] 5. Another Sort of *Thermoscope* is thus contrived. A and B are two Cylindrical Glass Vessels joined to the *Recurve Tube* D G F; the upper Part of the Vessel A is void of

Air,

Air, and the reſt is filled with ☿, as in the *Torricellian Experiment*, and the ☿ riſes half way in the Veſſel B. On the Surface of the ☿, there is put in a Tube ſome tinged Liquor, or rather *Oil of Tartar per Deliquium*, which will not Freeze, which reaches up to D, to the End of the Tube B K; a Glaſs Globe C full of *Air* is Sealed on *Hermetically*, to prevent Communication with the external *Air*. In this *Thermometer*, when by the Cold in the ambient Air, the Air C is cooled and condenſed; the ☿ will by its own Weight ſubſide in A, and riſe higher in B, and conſequently impel the Liquors up into the Tube B K; and if the *Baſis* of the Cylindrical Veſſel A and B be ten Times greater than the *Baſis* of the Tube B K; when the ☿ falls one Inch in A, or riſes one in B, the Liquor will riſe ten Inches in the Tube B K; alſo if the Air be heated in C, and rarified, it will by expanding it ſelf, make the ☿ deſcend in B, and riſe in A; ſo that the ſmalleſt Variations as to Heat and Cold are thus ſhewn by the Aſcent and Deſcent of the Liquor in the Tube B K.

To meaſure the Moiſture and Dryneſs of the Air, we uſe an Inſtrument called an *HYDROMETER* of which there are two or three Sorts.

Plate

Plate 4. *Fig.* 11.] 1. The First is made by a *Force-Balance*, in one of the Scales of which is put a Piece of Spunge, and in the other a Weight to Counterpoise it; the Spunge in damp Weather imbibes the Moisture and grows heavier. In dry Weather the Moisture being exhaled, the Spunge becomes lighter: And so by the Motions of the Examen we find the Alteration of the *Air*, in respect of its Humidity. To make the Variations the more sensible, the Examen of the *Balance* is made very long, which passes on a circular *Arch* of *Brass* divided into Degrees, marked 1, 2, 3, &c. According as the End of the Examen is at any of these Degrees, so we judge of the Weather.

Plate 6. *Fig.* 2.] 2. Another Sort is contrived after this manner. To a Rope or Cat's-Gut, a Cylindrical Weight is tied; in damp Weather the Rope by twisting it self will contract and pull up the Weight, and in fair Weather lets it sink farther down. To make the Variations more sensible, the Cylindrical Weight being about fifteen or sixteen Inches round, is divided into thirty or forty equal Parts, marked 1, 2, 3, &c. To prevent its being injured a Glass is put over it, thro' which the String paſſes at A; this Glaſs is covered with Brown or Blew Paper, except one ſmall Hole, thro' which the Figure on the Side of the Weight may be ſeen. Now the twiſting or untwiſting of the Rope, according to the Variation of the Moiſtneſs of the *Air*, will always preſent a new Figure to the Hole.

Plate 6. *Fig.* 17.] 3. A third Sort of *H Y-D R O M E T E R* is made with the *Beard* of a wild *Oat*, or the *Husk* of a ſmall *Vetch*, which in dry Weather twiſts, and in wet Weather untwiſts. One End is faſtned to the Bottom of a *Box*, the other comes thro' an Hole in the Lid, and has an Index adapted to it, ſo that the Motion of the Hand or Index on the Top of the *Box* ſhews the Variation of the Moiſtneſs and Dryneſs of the Weather.

CATOPTRICKS.

DEFINITIONS.

1. RAYS of Light are those which are diffused every way in strait Lines thro' the same Medium, and spread themselves constantly after the same Tenor, as long as they continue in the same Medium.

2. A Radiant is that, from whose Points Rays disperse themselves every way.

3. *Diverging Rays* (Plate 7. Fig. 3.) are those which meet in a Point opposite to the Direction of their Motion, or those Rays which spread themselves after that manner, as if they had all come from one Point, whether they really came from that Point or not. As the Rays B D going from B to D, are said to diverge from the Point C, whether they actually come from it or not; for tho' they should come from A, they are said to diverge from C, because if you produce them from B till they meet in a Point opposite to the Direction of their Motion, that Point will be C.

4. Con-

4. *Converging Rays are those which meet, or being produced, meet in a Point towards that Part whither the Direction of the Motion tends. As the Rays D B are said to Converge towards C, whether they meet in C, or after Refraction thro' the Glass E E, they go on Parallel to the Line A C D.*

5. *The Focus is that Point where the Rays meet.*

6. *Parallel Rays are those which come from a Point at a great Distance from us, and contain but a very small Angle one with another, as from the Sun.*

7. *Rays are said to Reflect, when they are turned backward in the same Medium.*

A real Focus is the Place where the Rays actually meet, as (in Fig. 5.) *the Point B where the Rays D meet, after they have past the Glass C C, and the Point A, where these converging Rays wou'd meet, if there was no Glass at C C, is called the* Imaginary Focus.

Fig. 8. Plate 7.] *In a Concave Mirror, if e be an Object, E will be the Focus of the Rays, which having diverged from the Object, and fallen upon the Concave Mirror, are by Reflection made to Converge at E.*

Plate 7. Fig. 3.] *A Concave Glafs tranfmitting Light, has no real Focus of parallel Rays, becaufe after they have paffed the Glafs they diverge from one another, as the Rays A after they have paffed the Glafs E diverge towards D, but the Point C is called the* Vertical Focus of the Concave Glafs.

8. *The Angle of Incidence, is that which is contained under the incident Ray* (Fig. 2. Plate 7.) *and the ⊥ to the Plane of the Point of Incidence, as A B C.*

9. *The Angle of Reflection is that which is contained under the reflected Ray, and the faid ⊥ as the Angle D B C, fometimes A B E, and D B F, are called the* Angles of Incidence and Reflection.

THEOREME.

The Angle of Incidence *is always equal to that of* Reflection. *This is confirmed by Experience, and has been feveral ways Demonftrated by Mathematicians.*

10. *Specula, or Mirrors, are thofe which by reflecting of the Light form Images of external Radiants.*

THE-

THEOREME.

Plate 7. *Fig.* 1. *or* 4.] RAYS coming from a Point A, and falling on a plain Mirror B C, after Reflection diverge from the Point *a*, which is in the ⊥ as far behind the Glass, as the Radiant is before it. For because A B is equal to *a* and B, and D B is common to the Triangles A B D and *a* B D, and the Angles at B are equal, the Angles A D B and *a* D B will be equal, *per* 4*th El.* 1. But by the 15 of the same, the Angles D A B and G D C are equal; therefore, if A D be the incident Ray, G D will be the reflected. After the same manner it may be shewn that H E is the reflected Ray of the Incident A E and K F of A F; and therefore all the reflected Rays, if produced, will meet at *a*. If the Eye was placed at H, it would receive the Rays which come from A, and are reflected at the Surface B C, as if they had really come from *a*, and consequently the Eye will be the same way affected as if it came at O, *Fig.* 4. and received the Rays coming from A; and therefore the Eye at H will see the Image of the Point A at *a*.

Fig. 6.

Fig. 6. Plate 7.] Since the Image of every Point is as far behind the Glass as the Point is before the Glass, the Image must be the same way inclined to the Glass as the Radiant is. So the Image of the Point A must be at *a*, and the Image of the Point E must be at *e*.

Hence it follows, that if the Glass lies horizontally, Objects will have their Images inverted, and Men will appear with their Heads downwards, as when we look in the Water.

What has been shewn of the principal Radiants, is also true of their Images; for they may be considered as Objects which send Rays; and therefore if there be another Glass to receive these Rays, there will be another Image formed within that Glass, and so that Image will still have another Image, &c. From whence arises the Multiplication of Images by the help of two or three plain Looking-Glasses.

Plate 7. Fig. 7.] Suppose two Looking-Glasses B C E F, let the Radiant be A, whose Image by the Glass B C is *a*; this Image being considered as a Radiant, will send Rays to the Glass E F at *a*, and this Image will likewise have its Image in the Glass B C at G, and so you may multiply Images

as

as far as you please. If G D H E K F (*Fig.* 4.) be incident *Rays*, their reflected *Rays* will be D A, E A, F A, *i. e.* if *Rays* be converging to the Point *a*, there to form an Image; and there be interposed a plain Speculum B, they will reflect to the Point A and Form an Image there. Experience answers to this exactly.

Fig. 9.] Take common *Reading* or *Burning Glass* E, and put the Radiant at A. Let the Place of the Image to be formed be *a*, put a *Looking-Glass* at B C, and a Man's Eye at O will see the Image at *a* in the Air between him and the Glass; for by the *Burning-Glass* the Rays coming from a Point in the Radiant A are made to Converge to a correspondent Point in the Image *a*; but by the *Looking-Glass* they are intercepted and reflected, therefore they will be turned another way, and those that went from one Point at A will meet with another correspondent to it at *a*, where they will form an Image.

In Concave Spherical Mirrors the Image of any Point is always in a Line passing thro' that Point and the Center.

Plate 7. *Fig.* 10.] Thus the Image of the Point E will be at *e*, the Image of F at *f*, and the Image of G at *g*. Hence

Hence it follows, that if the Image be in the Air before, it will appear inverted. The Reason why the Image is formed, is, becaufe all the *Rays* which come from the Point E, and falling near the Vertex of the Mirror, reflect fo, that they will meet at *e*, whence they diverge, forming at *e* the Image of the Point E. After the fame manner thofe which come from F after Reflection meet again at *f*, and there form the Image of F.

If the Radiant approaches the Glafs, the Image will recede from the Glafs, and at the Center of the Sphere they will both meet.

If the Radiant approaches ftill nearer, the Image will go out beyond the Center; and when the Radiant comes to be at the diftance of a quarter of the Diameter from the Vertex, the Image will be out at an infinite diftance. When the Radiant comes nearer to the Glafs than a quarter of the Diameter, the Image appears behind the Glafs, and erected. If the Mirror be Convex, the Image of an external Radiant is always behind the Glafs.

Plate 7. *Fig.* 8.] The Magnitude of the Image may be known from this; that it always appears under the fame Angle from the Vertex of the Speculum that the Radiant does, and consequently they will have the same Proportion one to another as their Distances from the Vertex have; and therefore if the Radiant be farther off than the Distance from the Glass, it will be bigger than the Image, if at the same Distance at the Center they are equal; if the Image is farther off than the Radiant from the Glass, it will appear bigger than the Radiant. See the Figure where E may be the Radiant, and *e* the Image; or *e* the Radiant and E the Image.

N. B. *The Focus or Point where the Image is formed, is the middle Point between the Vertex and Center of the Speculum; in all these Cases where the Radiant is supposed at an infinite Distance, as the Sun, and the Rays sent from it are reckoned as Parallel.*

DIOP.

DIOPTRICKS.

WHEN a *Ray* of Light comes out of one Medium into another, it changeth its Direction. This changing of the Direction is what we call *Refraction*.

Plate 7. *Fig.* 12.] The Angle of *Refraction* is comprehended under the refracted Ray, and a ⊥ drawn to the Surface of the refracting Medium, at the Point where the incident Ray falls on the same Medium as the Angle H D K. If the Ray of Light goes into a thicker Medium, it comes nearer to a ⊥; if into a thinner, then it recedes from the ⊥.

Fig. 11.] There are several ways to shew this by Experience. *V. G.* Take a *Bason*, into which put a Piece of Money at A, and then recede so far back, that the Sides of the *Bason* may intercept the Sight, so that the Light cannot come in a strait Line from A to the Eye at D; if Water be afterwards poured in, the Money will be seen; for the Ray A B when it comes to the Surface of the

Air at B, changeth its Direction, and goes off in D B, and so enters the Eye.

Fig. 12. *Plate* 7.] Suppose the Medium E C to be Air, H K Glass or Water, and A B the Surface of the Medium H K. Let E D be a Ray of Light, entering the Medium at D, as the Angle E D C is the Angle of Incidence, so is H D K the refracted Angle, and the Sides of these Angles have always a certain determinate Proportion to one another; and if you take small Angles, they themselves are always in this Proportion. If E C be Air, and H K Glass, the Angle E D C is to H D K, as 3 to 2. If E C be Air and H K Water, the Proportion between the Angles E D C and H D K is as 4 to 3.

Fig. 13.] To shew Refraction more plainly, take a common *Burning-Glass*, and cover it with Paper, in which let there be two Holes, thro' which the Light is to pass at B and C, then put a Candle at A; the Light passed thro' without bending the Rays coming thro' the Holes B and C, ought to diverge farther and farther from one another; but we find that if the Light be received on a Piece of Paper, the Rays converge one to another; when the Paper is at I, the Light falls at G K; when

when it's removed farther, the Rays fall at D E nearer one another, and when the Paper is removed to F, there the two Lights coincide and then diverge again.

Plate 8. *Fig.* 4.] Suppose G H Water, I A F Air, the Rays coming out of Water into Air are refracted, so that those which came from the Point E, seem after Refraction as if they had come from C, and enter the Eye at I A, as if they had all come from that Point. So that C E is a quarter of B E.

Fig. 3. *Plate* 8.] Hence when we look on an Object in Water, it appears a quarter nearer the Surface than it is; and on the same Account an Oar in the Water will appear bent, for the Point A will appear higher, *viz.* at B, and the Point C at D; so that the Oar in the Water instead of being seen in the Position F C A, will be seen in that of F D B.

Plate 10. *Fig.* 6.] If the Object A be seen thro' the Prism G H, by the Eye at D, it will appear as if it was at C; for the Rays falling from A obliquely upon the Surface of the Prism at H, are refracted towards the ⊥ E (because they go from Air into Glass) and would go on still in

the

the *Direction* H G if they continued to move in Glafs, but emerging out of Glafs into Air, they are refracted from the ⊥ to F, and going on in the Line D G, enter the Eye as if they came directly from C.

If the fame Object be feen thro' a Medium which terminated by many plain different Surfaces, it will appear to be multiplied into as many as there are Surfaces, for thro' every Surface the Object is feen in a different Place; and confequently as many Surfaces as there are, fo many diftinct Objects will appear. The Rays which come from the Objects thro' thefe different Surfaces of the Glafs forming the Images therein on different Parts of the Retina.

A *Lens* is a Glafs which is terminated by two Spherical, or one Plain and one Spherical Surface.

And it is Convex on both Sides, or Convex on one Side, and Flat on the other.

Concave on both Sides, or Concave on one Side, and Flat on the other.

Or a *Menifcus*, that is, Concave on one Side, and Convex on the other.

Plate 10. *Fig.* 5.] When Rays diverge from any Point of an Object, and fpread themfelves e-
very

very way, if then you expose a *Convex-Lens* to these Rays, they will form a Cone, whose Vertex is at the Point of Divergence, and Base at the *Lens*; as the Rays which diverge from A, and fall on the Glass C D; when these Rays pass thro' the Glass they are all refracted (except that which falls at E on the Middle of the Glass) and meeting again at the Point B, form another *Cone* whose *Base* is the Glass C D (on the other Side) and Vertex at B: This *Cone* together with the other *Cone* is called a *Pencil of Rays*, and A E D is the *Axis* of the Pencil, or a Line drawn from the Point of Divergence on the Side of the Glass, to the Point of Divergence on the other. There are as many Pencils of Rays thro' a Glass as there are visible Points in the Object, and tho' the *Axis* of the oblique Pencils suffer some Refraction in passing obliquely thro' the *Lens*, yet they are not to be looked upon as refracted, because after they have passed the Glass, they go on in a Line H, *Fig.* 5. to the Line in which they moved before they entered it, and the thinner the *Glass* is, the more insensible is that *Refraction*.

Plate 8. *Fig.* 1.] *A a*, *B b*, *C c*, represent three Pencils of Rays passing thro' a double *Con-*

vex-Glafs. When the Object A B C by means of a double *Convex-Glafs* has its Image projected at at *b c a*; the *Angles* which the *Axis* of thefe Pencils that come from the Extremities of the Object make with the Middle of the *Glafs*, determine the Magnitude of that Image; and the Place where the Pencils of Rays terminate on thefe *Axes*, is called the *Diftinct Bafe*, becaufe there only is the moft *Diftinct Image* of the Object projected.

Plate 8. Fig. 1.] By the former *Experiment* it was fhewn, that the Light which comes from a certain Point in the Candle, placed at a due Diftance from the *Glafs* or *Lens*, was made by Refraction to converge and meet at a Point; therefore if there be an Object placed before the *Glafs* at A B C, all the Rays which come from the Point A will after Refraction be made to converge at the Point *a*, and all the Rays which come from B will after Refraction meet at *b*, and all the Rays which come from C will be refracted to *c*; and if the Eye be at *a*, it will receive the Rays diverging from the Points *a b c*, the fame way as if it had received the Rays directly coming from the principal Radiants A B C; and therefore the Image will be formed at *a b c* and inverted.

If

If a piece of Paper be placed at *a b c*, the Rays will thence be reflected by the Paper, and will Point on the Paper the *Image* of the Radiant.

The *Image* and the Radiant have always the same Proportion the one to the other, that their Distances from the *Lens* have; and therefore if the *Image* be farther from the *Lens* than the Radiant is, it will be bigger than the Radiant is; if nearer it will be less. If the Radiant at A B C be brought nearer to the *Lens*, the *Image* will recede farther from it; and it may be brought to such a determinate Distance, as to cast the *Image* as far from the Glass as may be required to magnifie it to any given Proportion. If the Glass be equally Convex on both Sides, and the Radiant placed at a Semidiameter's distance from the *Lens*, the *Image* is cast out at an infinite Distance; and if the Radiant be placed at an infinite Distance, the *Image* is at a Semidiameter's distance from the *Lens*.

If the *Sun* be the Radiant which is at an infinite *Distance*, and the *Glass* be sufficiently broad; in the Place of the *Image* there will be a Flame, which will burn very intensely, because all the Rays which come directly from the *Sun*, and fall on the broad *Lens*, are by Refraction brought into a small Space to form the *Image*.

Plate 8. *Fig.* 6.] If at the Place of the *Sun's Image* (which is sometimes called the *Focus* of parallel Rays, or sometimes simply the *Focus*) there be placed a Lucid Body, as a Candle or Lamp, the Rays, after Refraction thro' the *Lens*, will go out parallel, and not diverge from one another; and the Light not spreading, will continue in the same Intenseness at all *Distances*, and consequently it will illuminate Objects at a distance. On this Principle *Convex-Lanthorns* are made.

If the Radiant be nearer the *Lens* than the *Focus* of parallel Rays, the *Image* will not be seen on the other Side of the *Lens*, but on the same Side that the Radiant is, only farther of, and not inverted, but erect.

Fig. 5.] Suppose A B C a Radiant nearer to the *Lens* than the *Focus* of parallel Rays, all the Rays which come from the Point, A, will enter the Eye at E, as if they had come from the Point *a*; and all the Rays which come from B and C will seem to have diverged at first from *b* and *c*; and so the Eye will see the Object not at A B C, but at *a b c*; and because the Angle D E D is the same with *a* E *c*, the *Object* will be seen magnified, *a b c* being greater than A B C.

If

If a *Room* be darkned, and only one Hole made in the Window to let in the *Rays* which come from external *Objects*, and in the Hole there be placed a *Convex Lens*, this *Lens* will form the *Images* of all external *Objects* that are before it; and if at a distance there be put a Piece of white Paper, the *Images* will be received on it, and they will all appear inverted: The Reason of which follows plainly from the former Principles; for all the *Rays* which come from any one Point of the *Object*, will by Refraction be made to meet at one Point on the Paper, and thence they will be reflected again; and the same thing is true of every other Point: So that the *Image* of every Point thus put together on the Paper will shew the *Image* of the radiant Object in the same Colour the Object is of, because every *Image* is formed by the very same Rays, and of the very same Affection as to Colour, as they which come from the Objects are. The Objects being much farther from the *Lens* than the *Images* are, these must be much less, and the nearer the Object is to the *Lens*, the *Image* will be the farther from it, and appear the bigger.

If the Object move, the *Image* will also seem to move; provided it do not move directly towards the *Lens*. By this Principle the Prospect of Places may be taken.

Plate 7. *Fig.* 14.] The Appearances of the *Magick Lanthorn* differ but little from those of the dark Chamber. The *Lanthorn* has two *Convex-Glasses* at A and B B, and a *Lamp* burning; at F there is a Slit made to hold a long Piece of Wood D C, in which are cut several round Holes to hold the *Pictures* which are of painted *Glass*; and the Flame of the Candle or Lamp E being great, a considerable Quantity of Light falls on the *Pictures*, and passing thro' the two Lens's, will form the Images of these *Pictures* on the opposite Wall: The *Pictures* being much nearer to the *Lens* than their *Images* on the Wall, the *Images* will be prodigiously larger than the *Pictures*, according as the Wall is distant. If by pulling out the Tube in which the *Lens* B is fixed, you make the Distance from the *Pictures* greater, the Distance of the *Images* will be less, and consequently the *Images* themselves will be less in proportion.

Plate

Plate 8. *Fig.* 13.] A *Concave Lens* forms the *Image* on the same Side that the *Radiant* is, but much less and nearer it. For if the *Object* B A be put before the *Lens* E F, it will be seen by the *Eye* at C, in the Position *a b*, and by consequence less than the *Object*; for the *Ray* A E falling on the *Lens* at E, is refracted into *g* E, and comes nearer to the ⊥, and the *Ray* E *g* coming on the Convex Surface of the *Air* at *g*, will be refracted into *g c* and recede from the ⊥: So that the *Rays* A B will enter the *Eye* at C or *c*, as if it had come directly from *a*, and not from A. So that the *Eye* being at C, and receiving the *Rays* coming from A and B, will be the same way affected as if they came from *a* and B. After the same manner the *Rays* which come from B will enter the *Eye* at C, as if they had come from *b*, so that the *Eye* will see the *Object* B A at B *a* nearer to it, and also much less than it really is.

Plate 8. *Fig.* 8.] The *Eye* is a *Lens* contrived by GOD to project the *Images* of external Objects on the *Retina*; and then it is that we see distinctly, when those *Images* are distinctly painted on the *Retina*. Immediately under the first Coat of the *Eye*, which is called the *Tunica Cornea*, A B,

B, there's an Humour of the same Consistence with Water, and is called the Aqueous Humour E F. In the Middle of this there swims another *Membrane*, called the *Uvea* C D, which is opaque, and lets no Light pass thro' it, but as perforated at C D, and the small Hole is called the *Pupilla*; so that all the Light which forms the *Image* must pass thro' that Hole. Next to the watery Humour is a consistent Globe, which is called the Christalline Humour K, and behind this is placed the vitreous Humour H G, which is not consistent as the Christalline, but yet is firmer than the Aqueous. Behind the vitreous Humour lies the *Retina*, which arises from the Insertion of the Optick Nerve at L, and it is supposed to consist of an infinite Number of small Nerves, standing ⊥ by, on the Concave Surface of the *Eye*, on which the *Images* of external Objects are painted. The Figure of the *Eye* is Spherical, being the only Figure which can turn every way in the Hole it fills up.

Now because those *Rays* only which come from any single Point of an Object, and fall on the Middle of the *Eye* at M, are united at one Point on the *Retina*, those which fall at A and B obliquely, not being exactly united with the rest, at that

that Point, therefore the *Eye* is furnished with the *Uvea*, an opaque Coat, which intercepts all those *Rays* which fall obliquely on the *Eye*.

The *Pupilla* or Hole in this Coat, has Power to dilate or contract it self, to let more or less Light pass thro' it, and in the Day time it is but small; for too much Light from the Sun would hurt the *Eye*: In the Night time it grows wider, to let in all the Light it can to affect the *Retina*; and this is the Reason why at Twilight Things appear bigger than they are, for the *Pupilla* being very wide, a great many *Rays* come on the *Retina*, which fall on the Corner very obliquely, and therefore will not all be united in one Point on the *Retina*, but take some Space on it, and so the *Image* of the whole will be much greater than it ought to be. 'Tis on the same Account that a Candle, in the Night time, seen at a Distance, appears much greater than it ought to do, and the same is true of the fixed Stars, for they appear much less if we look at them thro' a small Hole in a Paper.

To make all this plain, take two Tin Tubes made to go one within the other, so that you might make them longer or shorter as you please;

if at one End of these Tubes was put a *Lens*, and at the other fastened a piece of oiled Paper, or any thin *Membrane* of an Animal to represent the *Retina*, and the End where the *Lens* is put, be covered with a Lid, in which must be made a small Hole to represent the *Pupilla*; then if you draw the *Retina* backwards or forwards, you will at a certain Distance see the *Images* of external Objects painted on it in their true Colours, as in the dark Chamber, or Magick Lanthorn.

Since then the *Eye* is a *Lens* which projects the *Images* of external Objects on the *Retina*, if the *Eye* should keep always the same Figure, and the *Retina* the same Distance behind it, there would be but one certain and determinate Distance at which it would see Objects distinctly; V G. If the *Retina* were just at the Distance of the *Focus* of *Parallel Rays* from the *Cornea*, no Objects would have their *Images* distinctly projected on the *Retina* but those which are at a good Distance from it, so long as the *Eye* kept that Figure; but if the *Eye* were of such a Figure, as to cast the *Images* of near Objects on the *Retina*; if the Objects were farther removed, the Images would not fall on the *Retina*, but between the *Cornea* and it. If then

then the *Eye* kept one and the same Figure always, there would be no distinct Vision, but when *Objects* are at one determinate Distance from the *Eye*, which would be very inconvenient for *Animals*: And therefore to remedy this, the *Eye* has the Power of changing its Figure, whereby the *Cornea* is sometimes part of the Surface of a larger Sphere, sometimes of a lesser, and it is on this Account that the *Eye* is made to consist of various and flexible Humours and Parts, the most moveable of all which is the watery Humour, lying immediately under the *Cornea*, next to which is the Christalline of the firmest Consistence; the Christalline is closely embraced by the *Ligamentum Ciliare*, by which it is suspended, and the Fibres of the Ligament by their Contraction or Dilatation bring the Christalline backwards or forwards. When the Christalline is brought forwards, it forwards the aqueous Humour, and makes the *Eye* more protuberant, or the Segment of a lesser Sphere: On the contrary, when the Christalline is brought back, the aqueous Humour returns also, and the *Eye* becoms more flat, or the Segment of a larger Sphere; so that by the Motion of the Christalline the *Cornea* is made more or less convex, the greatest

greatest Refraction being made on the *Cornea*. 'Tis by this Mobility or Changeableness of the *Eye* that we are made to see *Objects* at different Distances from us.

If the *Objects* are at a Distance, the *Eye* that looks at them grows flatter, if they are near us, the *Eye* grows more convex: Now if the *Eye* could apply it self to see *Objects* at all Distances from us, we could always see every *Object* distinctly, and near *Objects* would be brought so near the *Eye*, that we could see them magnified in any Proportion we pleased. For we estimate the Magnitude of Objects seen with one *Eye* by the Angle under which they appear: Thus the Object A B (*Plate* 8. *Fig.* 10.) appearing under the Angle A E B, its Image takes up the Space *a b* on the *Retina*, but the Object C D appearing only under the Angle C E D, its Image takes up only the Space *c d* on the *Retina*.

One and the same Object at different *Distances* from the *Retina*, will appear under very different Angles. Suppose A B (*Fig.* 11.) the Object, and the *Eye* at *c*, the Angle under which the Object appears, is the Angle A C B, if the same Object be removed to *a b*, the Angle under which it appears

appears is the *Angle a* C *b* if it be brought to *a b*, the *Angle* at the *Eye* is *a* C *b*, so that the *Angle* will still be greater the nearer the Object comes to the *Eye*.

Fig. 14.] Suppose then a small Object A B, which of the ordinary *Distance* at which the *Eye* lies, appears under the *Angle* A C B, which is so very small that the *Eye* can't perceive the Parts of the Object distinctly; if then the *Eye* were brought Ten or a Hundred times nearer V. G. to D, and if it could form it self to see distinctly at all *Distances*, it would appear to the *Eye* under the *Angle* A D B, Ten or a Hundred times bigger than A C B, and consequently the Object will appear Ten or a Hundred times magnified: But then tho' the *Eye* consisting of flexible Parts, can change its Figure so as to lie at several *Distances*, yet this Mutability of Figure consists within certain Limits, and there must be certain *Distances* in which an Object must be put to be seen distinctly; so that if the Object be put nearer the *Eye* than this determinate *Distance*, it can never be seen distinctly, the Image not falling on the *Retina*, but its Place would either be behind the *Retina*, if the Rays could go so far before they were intercepted, or the Image will be vertical and before the *Eye* if the Object were nearer than the *Focus* of Parallel Rays, and consequently it can't be painted on the *Retina*.

If there were any solid Bodies swimming in the aqueous Humour, those can never have the Images on the *Retina*, but their Images will be vertical and before the *Eye*. This is a Demonstration that the *Musca Volitantes* can never be produced by Objects swimming in the aqueous Humour, as Physicians generally imagined.

Plate 8. *Fig.* 17.] Since then the Object A B may be so near the *Eye* at D, that it will be without the Limits of distinct Vision; it's plain that it can't be seen magnified to the naked Eye in any given Proportion, which it would be, could the Eye see distinctly at all *Distances*; but if before the Eye D be put a *Lens* C E, which consists of Segments of small Spheres, and the *Distance* of the Objects from the *Lens* be less than the *Focus* of the Parallel Rays, the *Lens* will form the Image of the Object A B at *a b*; that is, all the Rays which come from the Points A and B will enter the Eye as if they had come from the Points *a b*, and the Eye will see the Object at *a b*, at the Distance

stance necessary for distinct *Vision*, and it will appear under the *Angle* A D B, or *a* D *b*, which is the very same that it would have been under to the naked Eye at D. If the Object were placed at the *Focus* of Parallel Rays, then all the Rays which come from the Point A after Refraction thro' the *Lens*, would go Parallel and enter the Eye as if they had come from an infinite *Distance*, so the Eye would see the Point A in the Line A *a* produced in *Infinitum*. The same thing is true of the Point B, and the Object would be seen at an infinite *Distance* under the *Angle a* D B, which is the very same under which it would be seen by the naked Eye, if it could see it at D distinctly.

Fig. 16. *Plate* 8.] Suppose an Object A B, which to the Eye at C the ordinary *Distance* for distinct Vision appears, under the small *Angle* A C B, if then I would see this Object an Hundred times magnified, I take a small *Lens* whose *Focal Distance* for Parallel Rays is an Hundred times less than A C or B C, and put the *Lens* at G, so that the *Distance* of the *Lens* from the Object may be a Hundred times less than the *Distance* of the Eye at C from the Object: If then I bring my Eye to D to the *Lens*, I shall see the Object thro' the

the *Lens* under the *Angle* A D B, which is a Hundred times greater than A C B, and the Eye will see the Object thus magnified distinctly, because it sees at a greater *Distance* from the Eye; for most Mens Eyes are framed to see Objects at a good *Distance* from the Eye distinctly.

Fig. 15. *Plate* 8.] If there were an Object A B and a *Lens* E, whose *Focal Distance* is F E, that Object would appear by the *Lens* under the *Angle* A E B: If there were a *Lens* whose *Focal Distance* is D F, the *Angle* under which the Object will appear will be A D B, greater than A E B; if there were another *Lens* at C, whose *Focal Distance* is C F, the *Angle* under which the Object would appear thro' this *Lens* is A C B, which is still greater than A D B. The less then the *Focal Distance* of Parallel Rays of any *Lens* is, the more 'twill magnify the Object. And if the *Lens* be equally convex on both Surfaces, the *Focal Distance* for Parallel Rays is a *Semidiameter's Distance* from the *Lens*; the less then the *Semidiameter* of the Sphere is, of whose Segment the *Lens* is made, the more it will magnify the Object; and the whole Art of magnifying Objects by single *Microscopes*, is to grind Glasses exactly of Portions

of

of very small Spheres. *Lewenhoeck* and *Melon* pretended to grind Glasses whose *Focal Distance* not much exceed the hundreth Part of an Inch. I have heard of some that are less, and if they were let fall on Paper, there would be need of another *Microscope* to find them with.

To know how much any of these single *Microscopes* magnify; take a small piece of Paper, suppose 'tis of an Inch *Diameter*, and paste it on a Wall; then take a *Microscope* and put any small *Object* at the *Focus* of Parallel Rays from it; then recede so far from the Wall, till the Paper on it appears of the same Bigness with the *Object* seen thro' the *Microscope*; then consider what Proportion the *Distance* of your Eye from the Paper on the Wall bears to the *Distance* of the *Object* from the *Microscope*, and in that Proportion the *Object* will be magnified, or appear greater than it would do were it placed at the same *Distance* from the Eye with the Paper on the Wall.

We may perform this more easily thus. Take a round piece of Paper of about two or three Inches *Diameter*, and dye it black with Ink, then paste it on a Pane of Glass in the Window and recede so far from it, till looking thro' the *Microscope* with

one

one Eye on the *Object*, and with the other on the Paper, you perceive them both of the same Bigness, or the one exactly to cover the other, the Proportion between the Paper and the *Object* will be exactly as the *Distance* of the *Object* from the *Microscope* to that of the Eye from the Paper; and consequently when the *Object* appears of the same bigness with the Paper, it is magnified in that Proportion.

Tho' most Mens Eyes have such a Flexibility and Changeableness of Figure, that they can't only see *Objects* at a great *Distance*, if they appear under any sensible *Angle*, but also those that are within two or three, or one Foot of their Eye, yet there are several whose Limits of *Distance* for distinct *Objects* as to their Vision, are much less. V. G. Some can't see *Objects* but when they are very near them, or close to their Eye, which being very convex, or the Segment of a small Sphere, will unite the Rays of *Objects* at a *Distance* before they come to the *Retina*. They who have this Fault in their Sight are called *Myopes*.

On the contrary, there are others whose Eyes are very flat, or Segments of large Spheres, who can't see unless the *Objects* be at a good *Distance* from them,

them, and the Rays which come from one Point to fall into the Eye are *quam proxime* Parallel —— Becauſe old Men have generally their Eyes very flat, ſo that they can't ſee but at a Diſtance; therefore thoſe who are troubled with this Fault, are called *Presbytæ*: Both their Faults of Viſion may be helpt by *Lens*'s; for thoſe who are Short-ſighted, and can't ſee any Object but what is very near them, by looking thro' a Concave Lens, will ſee diſtinctly Objects, which at the ſame Diſtance without the Lens, they could not ſee but very confuſedly.

Plate 8. *Fig.* 9.] Suppoſe the Object A B C, and the Eye of a *Myopes* at E, the Object being without the Limits of diſtinct Viſion, will be ſeen confuſedly by the Eye at E; but if you put in the Concave-Lens at G between the Object and the Eye all the Rays which come from it will enter the Eye as if they had come from *a*, which is much nearer to the Eye, and within the Limit of diſtinct Viſion; the ſame may be ſaid of B and C from this *Experiment*; therefore it's plain that by the help of ſuch a Lens, the Eye of a *Myops* will ſee diſtinctly the Object A B C tho' much leſs than if it had ſeen it without the Lens.

Plate 8. *Fig.* 12.] As a Concave-Lens makes Short-fighted People see more distinctly; so also the Convex-Lens helps off the Sight of a *Presbyta*; for suppose A B an Object, and the Eye at C, this Object is so near the Eye that it can't be seen distinctly by it. If therefore there be a Concave-Lens put at E, so that the Object may be within the *Focus* of Parallel Rays, the *Eye* will see the Object A B at *a b*, at a farther Distance, and within the Limits of distinct Vision; and it will see the Object take up the Space *a b* which is greater than A B, and therefore it will see it magnified; whereas an *Object* seen thro' a *Lens* fit for a *Myops* does always appear less.

Double Microscopes are those which consist of 2, 3, or 4 Lens's that are designed to magnifie the Object.

Plate 9. *Fig.* 1.] The first sort is made after this manner. C is a Lens of a small Sphere, before which the Object A B is placed at such a Distance, that the Image made by the Lens C may be cast out at a great Distance on the other Side, *viz.* at *a b*, so that if *a b* be 10 or 100 times farther from C than A B is, it will be 10 or 100 times greater than A B. D E is another Lens
which

which is larger and put so near the *Image a b*, that *a b* will be either in its *Focus* of parallel *Rays*, or somewhat nearer; so that the *Image* of the *Image a b*, made by the *Lens* D E, may be cast out at a distance, fit for distinct Vision. Now if the *Eye* be applied at G, it will see the the *Object* under the *Angle*, equal to the *Angle* E *f* D, and consequently magnified, and at a distance fit for distinct Vision.

Plate 9. Fig. 2.] Most of the double *Microscopes* now in use have three *Glasses*, and are made thus. C is the *Object Glass*, which is the Portion of a small *Sphere*; A B is the *Object* something farther than the *Focus* of parallel *Rays*; so that the *Image* may be cast out, and fill the Space *a b* 10 or 100 times greater than A B. D E is another *Lens* or *Segment* of a larger *Sphere* placed at a little distance from *a b*; to this join the Glass G H, which is the *Segment* of a *Sphere* somewhat less than D E: So that the Distance between the *Glasses* G H and D E, may be less than the Distance of the *Focus* of parallel *Rays* of the *Glass* G H, and that the *Rays* which come from the *Image a b*, may pass the two *Glasses*, and after Refraction enter the *Eye* at L. So that all those

Rays which come from the same Point of the *Image a b*, may enter the *Eye* as if they had come from an infinite Distance, *i.e.* the two *Glasses* G H and D E ought to be so placed, that the *Rays* which come from any one Point of the *Object a b*, may after Refraction thro' these two *Glasses* run parallel, and so form in the *Eye* a distinct *Image*; for it is plain, that in this Case the *Eye* will see the *Object* much magnified and distinct. By this *Microscope* the *Eye* can perceive a greater Portion of the *Object* than by the former; because the *Rays* at *b* and *a* would fall so obliquely on the *Glass* D E, that without the third *Glass* H G, they could not enter the *Eye*, and consequently without that *Glass* the *Eye* will see only the middle Part of the *Object*.

As *Microscopes* are used to discover the small Parts of these Bodies we have near us, and put at a due Distance from the *Microscope*: So *Telescopes* are for discerning Bodies distinctly that are at great Distance from us; so that the *Rays* which come from any one Point of the *Object*, and fall on the object *Glass* of the *Telescope*, may be conceived as Parallel, and consequently they will unite and form the *Image* as the *Focus* of parallel *Rays*.   *Plate*

Plate 4. *Fig.* 15.] The first and most simple Sort of *Telescope* is the *Astronomick*, for looking at the *Stars*. C D represents the object *Glass*, which is a Portion of a very large *Sphere*; A E and B E, are two *Rays* which come from the Extremities of an Object placed at a great Distance, as the Object A B is to be supposed. All the *Rays* which come from the same Point that A E came from, will after Refraction thro' the *Lens* meet at *a*, and all the *Rays* which come from the same Point of the Object with the *Rays* B E, will after Refraction meet at the Point *b*; so that the *Image* of the Object will be placed at *b a*, at the Distance of the *Focus* of parallel Rays, as you may see by the pricked Lines.

Suppose G F H a *Lens* of a much greater Convexity, or a *Segment* of a much larger *Sphere*; placed so near the *Image a b*, that *a b* may be in its *Focus* of parallel Rays, that is to say, all the Rays which come from the Points *a* and *b*, may after Refraction run parallel and enter the *Eye* at L, as if they had come from a great Distance; these *Lens*'s being thus adapted, and put in a *Tube*, the *Eye* will see distant Objects distinctly, and magnified in the Proportion that the focal *Di-*
stance

stance of the *Glass* C D, as greater than the focal *Distance* of G H. For first the *Eye* will see the Object distinctly, because the Rays which come from the Points *a b*, falling on the *Eye* at L, as if they had come from a great *Distance*, will be exactly united in the *Retina*, and therefore a distinct *Image*.

2*dly*. The Object will be seen much greater than without the *Telescope*, for the Angle under which the Object is seen without the *Telescope*, is the Angle A L B, and the *Image* under the *Retina* of the *Eye* is A B; but the Angle under which the Object is seen with the *Telescope* is the Angle G L H and the *Image* made then on the *Retina* is K; and therefore as much as this latter Angle and Image are greater than the former, so much is the Object magnified by the *Telescope*.

Again, let A and B be two Rays coming from the End of an Object at an infinite *Distance*, whose *Image* is *a b*, the bigness of which is determined by the Angle *a* E *b*, which these two Rays make in passing thro' the object *Glass*, without any Refraction, because they are the *Axes* of two Pencils of Rays: Let the focal Distance of the object *Glass* be E K, and that of the *Eye-Glass* F K, and

and A E B be the Angle under which the Object is seen without the *Telescope.* Now because the *Image* and the *Object* appear under the same *Angle* from the *Lens,* the *Angle* A E B will be equal to the *Angle* a E b, and consequently to the *Angle* under which the Object appears seen without the *Telescope*; but the Eye at L sees the *Image* a b under an *Angle* equal to a F b; and consequently so much greater as the *Angle* a F b is than a E b, so much greater will the Object appear when seen with the *Telescope* than when seen without it: But so much as E K is greater than F K, so much is the *Angle* a F b greater than a E b, *i. e.* the *Object* is magnified in proportion to the focal Distance of the object *Glass,* keeping the same *Eye-Glass*; and and consequently the longer the focal Distance, *i. e.* the longer the Space is, of which the *Lens* is a Portion, the more the Object will be magnified; and therefore the whole Perfection of these Sort of *Telescopes,* is to get object Glasses well ground of a long focal Distance. There are some of these *Telescopes* of 150 or 200 Feet in Length, but it is very difficult to manage and turn them as one pleases. It is plain, that the *Image a b* is inverted

ted in respect of the principal *Object*, and consequently whatever *Objects* we look at with these *Telescopes*, will appear inverted.

Plate 9. *Fig.* 4.] 2. *Galilæus's-Telescope* does likewise consist of two Glasses, whereof the object Glass is Convex, and a Segment of a lesser *Sphere*. They are fixed in a *Tube* after this manner. C D is the object Glass, whose Focus of parallel Rays is at *a b, i. e.* the *Images* of distant Objects made by the Glass C D are at *a b*, so that K is the Focus of parallel Rays to the *Axis* of the Glass; so that if it were not for the interposition of the *Eye-Glass* G H, all the Rays parallel to the *Axis* would converge to the Point K; but then by the interposition of the Concave *Eye-Glass* G H, which is placed at such a Distance from the *Image* *a b*, that the Point K is in its Focus of parallel Rays or vertical Focus, all the Rays which before they passed thro' the Glass G H were converging to the Point K, will after Refraction on the Glass G H, run parallel to the *Axis*: The same way all the Rays which before the Refraction on the Glass G H, were converging to the Points *a b*, will after Refraction run Parallel one to another. So that the *Eye* near F will receive all the Rays which were going to *a b*, as if they had all come from *a b* placed at a great diftance, and the *Eye* will fee the *Object* under the *Angle a* F *b* which is equal to *a* F *b*; where it is to be obferved that the *Image a b* is inverted in refpect of *a b*, and *a b* will be erected and feen the fame way that the principal *Object* A B is feen.

N. B. *The vertical Focus of a Concave Glafs is that Point from which the Rays parallel to the Axis diverge, after Refraction thro' the Glafs; as the Point C* (Plate 7. Fig. 3.) *is the vertical Focus of parallel Rays of the Glafs E E, becaufe the Rays B D, which come from A, and before they entered the Glafs were Parallel to the Axis A E, are by Refraction thro' the faid Glafs made to diverge from the Point C, as if they had come really from that Point.*

Plate 9. Fig. 5.] 3. Becaufe the firft Sort of *Telefcopes* fhew all *Objects* inverted, and the fecond difcovers but the fmall Part of an *Object* at once; therefore a third Sort has been contrived, confifting of four Glaffes, *viz.* one large *Object* Glafs and three *Eye-Glaffes,* placed after this manner. C D is the *Object-Glafs,* whofe Focus of parallel Rays is at *a b*: or which is the fame thing, let *a b* be the *Image* of some distant *Object*, therefore it will be inverted in respect of the *Object*. E F is an *Eye-Glass*, a *Segment* of a lesser *Sphere*, placed so near the *Image a b*, that Rays which come from any one Point of it after Refraction thro' E F, may run parallel, and fall on a third Glass G H; those parallel Rays falling on the Glass G H, will after Refraction converge to the Focus of parallel Rays, and form an *Image a b* inverted in respect of *a b*, and consequently erected in respect of the principal Radiant. I K is another Glass placed so near the *Image a b*, that the Rays coming from any one Point of the *Image a b* may enter the *Eye* at L, as they had come from a Point at a great Distance; that is, they will after Refraction at I K run parallel, and then the *Eye* at L will see the Image distinctly erected and magnified.

OBSERVE, that *a b* is the common Focus of parallel Rays to the two Glasses C D and E F, and *a b* is the Focus of parallel Rays to the two Glasses G H and I K.

Sir

Sir ISAAC NEWTON's
COLOURS.

PROPOSITION.

Lights which differ in Colour, differ also in Degrees of Refrangibility.

EXPERIMENT.

IF you apply any flat Side of a Prism to the Hole of a dark Room to receive the Rays which come from the Sun, these Rays which are different in Colour, will be separated by a different *Refraction*, and diverge from one another, (as in *Fig.* 1. *Plate* 10.) and appears distinctly in an oblong Figure on the opposite Wall: They will be refracted in this Order, *viz.* The red Rays will be refracted least,

the Orange somewhat more, the Yellow more than that, the Green yet more, the Blue more than the Green, and the Purple most of all. Now to shew that these Colours were not made by Refraction, but were originally in the Rays of the *Sun*; if you refract any one of them never so much with a Prism, as for *Example*, the Purple in the first Figure, it will retain the same Colour.

If you contract these refracted Rays with a Burning-Glass, they will all converge to the *Focus* of parallel Rays, as in the second Figure; where if you receive them on Paper, they will appear White: And to shew farther, that White is a Composition of all these *Colours*, if you intercept the blue Ray with a Piece of Paper, between the *Focus* and the Glass, the White at the *Focus* will appear Reddish; if the Reddish be intercepted it will appear Blueish. So that if one of these *Colours* is wanting, the White is imperfect.

Fig. 3. If you receive all the Rays on a Piece of Paper, as at L, *Figure* 3*d.* between the *Focus* of parallel Rays and the Glass, they will appear with their proper *Colours* in their right Order, and converging towards one another; but if they be received beyond the *Focus*, they will appear in
their

their proper *Colours* on the Paper, and to have diverged from one another, whence their Order will be inverted, *viz.* the purple Ray will be in the Place of the Red, and the Red of the Purple.

To shew that the Rays which differ in *Colour*, tho' they have the same Incidence, are differently refracted, place a tall Piece of Wood with an Hole in it, *Fig.* 4. and a Prism behind that Hole at a convenient Distance from the Window; then with it refract the several Rays one after another from the Hole in the dark Room, to the Hole in the Piece of Wood, and each of the Rays will be differently refracted on the opposite Wall. *Viz.* The *Reddish* will be least refracted, and uppermost; the *Orange* next, underneath; the *Yellow* next, the *Green* next, the *Blue* next, and the *Purple* lowest of all.

Those *Objects* whose Parts are so disposed, as to reflect any one of these Rays more than the rest, and in a great measure to absorbe and stifle the others, appear to be of that *Colour* which they most reflect; whence a blue *Ray* when refracted on a blue *Object*, appears much stronger than when it is refracted on one of a different *Colour*, and so of the rest. If you look thro' a Prism on an *Object*

ject of any one Particular, *V. G. Green*, you will see it in all the other *Colours*; but the *Green* being the moſt powerful, the *Object* to the Sight of the naked *Eye* will appear altogether of that *Colour*.

Since *White* has been proved to confiſt of all *Colours*; it follows from hence, that thoſe *Objects* which appear *White* to us, are ſuch as are diſpoſed very curiouſly to reflect all *Colours*, and the greater or leſs this Diſpoſition is in the Superficies of the *Object*, it will appear accordingly of a quite White, or elſe of a ſomewhat ſhaded Dark-brown, or ſome other intermediate *Colour*; and thoſe *Objects* which are very little, or not at all diſpoſed to reflect theſe *Rays*, will appear Black.

It may be ſo contrived by darkening a Room, and by that means letting Beams of Light fall very forcibly upon a black *Object*, that it ſhall then appear exactly White to the *Eye*.

If you expoſe two Pieces of Marble to the Sun, one White, the other Black, the Black will be hot, and retain the Heat longer; for as the White reflects, ſo the Black abſorbs the *Rays* of the Sun.

If

[191]

If an oblong Piece of Paper placed before a Window, be viewed at such a Distance thro' a Prism, that the Light from the Window on the Paper may make an Angle, equal to that which is made by it, *i.e.* the Light reflected from the Paper to the *Eye*, *Provided* the Paper be terminated with Sides parallel to the Prism, and the Horizon, and distinguished by a perpendicular transverse Line into two Halves, the one of an intensely blue *Colour*, the other intensely Red: If the refracted Angle of the Prism (*i.e.* its two Sides thro' which the Light passes to the *Eye*) be turned upwards, so that the Paper may seem to be lifted upwards by the Refraction, its blue Half will be lifted higher by the Refraction, than its red Half; but if it be turned downwards, so that the Paper may seem to be carried lower by the Refraction, its blue Half will be carried something lower thereby than its red Half; because in both Cases the Light which comes from the blue Half of the Paper thro' the Prism, to the *Eye*, is more refracted than that which comes from the red Half.

A

A Description of the Condensing ENGINE with its Apparatus.

PLATE 6.

Fig. 6. IS a *Syringe* or *Syphon* for injecting Air into the Veſſel *a a a a* of *Fig.* 10.

Fig. 9. A *Mercurial-Gage* made with a Glaſs Tube *c c* fixed into a Piece of Wood, to know by the riſing of the *Mercury* in the Veſſel *a a a a*.

Fig. 7. *b b b b* repreſent the *Braſs* Hemeſpheres; *g*, a *Cock* to keep the injected Air from coming out; *e e*, a hollow Piece of *Braſs* thro' which the Air is injected; *d d* a *Braſs* Plate to ſhut up the bottom of the Veſſel *a a a a*; *a* one of the *Braſs* Rings to hang the Weights on to draw the *Hemiſpheres* aſunder.

Fig. 10. *k*, the other *Braſs* Ring for the abovementioned purpoſe; *a a a a* is a Glaſs Veſſel

sel armed with *Brass* Hooks at *c*, the better to keep in the Air condensed upon the *Hemispheres* *b b b b* within the said Glass. *f*, a Piece of Brass screwed to the upper Hemisphere to sustain it by help of the Pieces *e, e, g,* hanging upon the Hook *k*, whilst the Weights in the Scale draw the lower Hemispheres from it, and without letting out the condensed Air. *h, h*, a Board with two screwed Pillars to fix the upper and lower Brass Plates to the Brass Vessel, *d, d,* the upper Brass Plate represented in *Fig.* 8. with the Collar of Leathers *f, f,* that the Piece *e, e,* of *Fig.* 7. may slip up and down without letting out the Air.

If the Air be exhausted out of the Hemispheres (joined only by a wet *Leather*) it will require thirty Pounds to draw them asunder; if the Density of the Air in the Vessel *a a a a* be doubled by the Quantity of injected Air on the outside of the Hemispheres, tho' the Air is not drawn out from between them, it will require as much Weight to draw them asunder, as before; and double that Weight if there is a *Vacuum* between the Hemispheres; or if the Air is three times as dense as at first. And if the Air being three times as dense as at first, there be *Vacuum* between the

Hemispheres, it will require three times the Weight, namely three hundred and ninety Pound to pull them asunder.

A Description of Rowley's Horary, or a Machine to represent the Motion of the Moon about the Earth, and the Earth, Venus and Mercury about the Sun.

THIS *Movement* represents that Part of the *Planetary System*, according to *Copernicus*, which is circumscribed by the *Earth*'s Motion round the *Sun*, or contain'd within the Orbit that the *Earth* describes about the *Sun*.

The flat *Silver* Ring which incompasses the whole Work upon the upper Face of the *Movement*, represents the *Plane* of the *Ecliptic*, and is divided into twelve equal Parts, which are the twelve

twelve *Signs* of the *Zodiac*; each Part is again subdivided into thirty equal Parts, which are the *Degrees* of each *Sign*, there being three hundred and sixty of these in the whole Circumference. This *Plane* of the *Ecliptic* passes thro' the *Sun*'s Centre, and the *Earth*'s Centre is carried round the *Sun* in the same *Plane*; so that no Body can be in a direct Line between the Centres of the *Earth* and *Sun*, unless that Body be in the *Plane* of the *Ecliptic*, it taking its Name from *Eclipses*, which never happen but when the *Moon* is in or near this *Plane*.

The Places of all the *Planets* are determined by their Situations in respect to the *Signs* of the *Zodiac*, beginning to reckon from *Aries*, and by their being in or out of the *Plane* of the *Ecliptic*; their Distance in *Degrees* from the beginning of *Aries* is their *Longitude*, and their Distance from the *Plane* of the *Ecliptic*, either above or below it, is their *Latitude*, which is either *Northern* or *Southern*, according as the *Planet* is towards the *Northern* or *Southern* Part of the *Ecliptic*.

Each primary *Planet* moves in an Orbit, whose *Plane* passes thro' the *Sun*'s Centre; and since only the *Earth* of all the primary *Planets* moves in the *Ecliptic*, every one of the other muſt conſequently paſs thro' the *Plane* of the *Ecliptic* at two oppoſite Points call'd *Nodes*.

The *Moon* moves in an Orbit, whoſe *Plane* paſſes thro' the *Earth*'s Centre. The two oppoſite Points where the ſaid Orbit cuts the *Plane* of the *Ecliptic*, being the *Moon*'s *Nodes*, which are repreſented in the *Machine* by two *Studs*; and ſince the *Nodes* are always in the *Plane* of the *Ecliptic*, if the *Moon* happen to be in either of them, when they are in a *Line* with the *Sun* and *Earth*, there will be an *Eclipſe*; 'twill be of the *Moon*, if the *Earth* is between the *Sun* and *Moon*, and of the *Sun*, if the *Moon* is between the *Sun* and *Earth*.

The Centre of each *Planet*'s Orbit not being in the *Sun*'s Centre, its Diſtance from it is called the *Excentricity*; upon this Account the *Planets* recede from, and approach towards the *Sun* at different times.

Theſe

These Deffinitions being premised.

The large gilt *Ball* in the Centre reprefents the *Sun*, which you may obferve to turn round upon a fix'd Axis, inclined to the *Plane* of the *Ecliptic*, in an Angle of about Eighty-two *Degrees* or eight *Degrees* diftance from a Perpendicular.

The innermoft fmall *Ball* is the Planet *Mercury*, which revolves round the *Sun* in an excentrick Orbit, with a proper *Degree* of *Inclination* to the Plane of the *Ecliptic*.

The next fmall *Ball* is *Venus*, commonly called the *Evening* or *Morning-Star*, which here revolves round in an Orbit of due *Inclination* and *Excentricity*.

The outermoft painted *Ivory Ball* reprefents the *Earth*, which revolves round the *Sun* in its proper Orbit, and at the fame time has a fwifter *Rotation* upon a *Steel* Axis, which Axis always ftands inclined to the *Plane* of the *Ecliptic* in an Angle of Sixty-fix and half *Degrees*, or Twenty-three *Degrees* and half from a Perpendicular, and points the fame way during the whole *Revolution*, it being always parallel to one and the fame *Line*;

Line; that is, if a fix'd *Star* be supposed at an immense Distance, the *Earth* shall always point to it, what Part soever of its Orbit is in the two Extremities of this Axis; namely where it goes into, and where it comes out of the Globe, represents the two *Poles*; the upper-most is the *North*, the opposite the *South Pole*; the other *Ball* which accompanies the *Earth* in its *Motion* round the *Sun*, and at the same time revolves round the *Earth*, represents the *Moon*, whose Orbit is less than that of the *Earth*, and has its proper *Degree* of *Inclination*.

The *Hemisphere* of *Mercury* or *Venus*, which is turned towards the *Sun*, is always enlightened, and the opposite *Hemisphere* dark, which is here represented by the white and black Part of the *Balls*.

It is to be observed of the *Moon*, that it turns once round its own Axis, whilst it is carried round the *Earth* in its own Orbit, which is performed in Twenty-seven Days and eight Hours; and therefore the same Face is always towards the *Earth*, and it is hereby expressed by the white Part of the *Moon* which is always towards the *Earth* in this *Machine*; but as it is not always enlightened, there is a dark Cap which expresses the

shaded

shaded Part of the *Moon*, or the Part not enlightned by the Sun, and thereby is exhibited how much is enlightened of that Part of the *Moon* which we see from the *Earth*; that is, what *Phasis* or Appearance the *Moon* has at any time.

Whereby is shewn how far any Part of the *Earth* moves round in a determinate Number of Hours.

The Circle on the *Moon*'s Orbit is divided into Twenty-nine Parts and half, which represents the Days of the *Moon*'s Age, that being the Period from New *Moon* to New *Moon*. The Number in the small Circle adjoining to the *Moon*'s Orbit, represents the Number of *Moons* or *Lunar-Months*.

The Number which appears in a small Hole made on the great gilt *Plate* shews the Year.

From these Measures of Time you will find the *Sun* revolves upon his Axis in about 25 Days.

Mercury revolves round the *Sun* in about 87 Days, 23 Hours.

Venus revolves round the *Sun* in about 224 Days, and 18 Hours.

The *Earth* revolves about the *Sun* in 365 Days 6 Hours, and about its own Axis in 24 Hours.

And

And the Nodes of the *Moon* have a retrograde *Revolution* in her Orbit in about 18 Years and 224 Days.

All which Motions nearly agree with those in the Heavens.

So that if this *Movement* be set to any given Time, so as to represent the Situations of the *Earth*, *Sun*, and *Planets*, in respect to each other, and be afterwards set a going, it will then truly represent the Situation of the *Planets*, with regard to each other for any given Time, past or to come. Only this you must observe, that the Proportion of the Orbs of the *Planets*, in respect of the Bulks of the Bodies, and the Proportion of their Bulks to each other, could not be performed in so small a Model as this is; but that may in some Measure be remedied by making the following Allowances.

Suppose the Diameter of the *Moon*'s Orb to be sixty Diameters of the *Earth*, and the Diameter of the *Earth*'s Orb round the *Sun* 300 times the Diameter of the *Moon*'s Orb, and the Orbs of *Venus* and *Mercury* to bear the same Proportion to the *Earth*'s, as they do in this *Machine*.

Then

Then for the Bodies, imagine the *Earth* to be in Diameter a little more then 3 times and half greater than the *Moon*, or in Bulk near 51 times. Suppose *Venus* about as large as our *Earth*, and *Mercury* about as large as the *Moon*.

And Lastly, Suppose the *Sun* to be near 100 times larger in Diameter than the *Earth*, that is in Bulk one Million of times larger.

F I N I S.

BOOKS

Printed for, and Sold by B. Creake, at the *Bible* and *Ink-Bottle* in *Jermyn-Street*, St. *James*'s; and J. Sackfield, in *Lincolns-Inn-Square*.

THE Mandate of his Eminence, Monseigneur, the Cardinal *de Noailles* Arch-bishop of *Paris*, in *French* and *English*, with the Act of Appeal, and Extract of the Registers of the Chancery, the Church, and University of *Paris*, of the 11th of *Sept.* 1718. As also the Extracts of the Register of the Conclusion of the Metropolitan Church of *Paris*, from the *Paris* Edition, put out by the Cardinal's Order. Just Publish'd. Price 1 *s*.

An Essay towards the Cure of *Religious Melancholy*, in a Letter to a Gentlewoman afflicted with it: Penn'd for her Use, and Publish'd at her Request. Price Bound 2 *s*.

Geography Epitomiz'd, or, *The London Gazetteer*: Or, A Geographical Historical Treatise of *Europe*, *Asia*, *Africa*, and *America*, with their several Empires, Kingdoms, Principalities, States, Provinces, Islands, Counties, Bishopricks, and chief Cities of the World; describing their Situations, &c. with an Account of the Inhabitants,

CATALOGUE.

their Behaviour, Manners, Politicks, Religion, &c. Rivers, Production of Soil, Rarities, Nature, and Riches: Likewise, their Revenues, Government, Force, Antiquities; with a Discription of K. *George*'s Dominions in *Germany*. To which is added, An Introduction to Geography, and Knowledge of the Globes and three Tables, &c.

A Geographical and Historical Account of the several Empires, Kingdoms, Republicks, and Sovereignty's of *Europe*; with an exact List of all the Capital Cities, Universities, Primaces, Archbishopricks thereof, with the Names of the respective Princes, their Ages, Issue, Parents, Relations, Religion, Alliances, Titles and Pretensions; together with an Account of the most Noted Sea-port Towns upon Navigable Rivers, and Strong Places. A Design as New as it is Useful for all those who desire to have any Knowledge of the Present State of *Europe*. Pr. 1 s.

Memoirs of the Life of Sir *Stephen Fox*, Knt. from his first Entry upon the Stage of Action under the Lord *Piercy*, till his Death, with many curious Incidents and Passages, not mention'd in the Lord *Clarendon*'s History, in the Reigns of the Kings, *Charles* and *James*, the 2d. K. *William*, and Q. *Anne*, and the two first Years of K. *George*; with an Account of his diffusive Charities and Benedictions, as also his last Will and Testament, his Legacies bequeath'd to his Relations and Friends. A Copy of the Schedule annex'd to his Will, faithfully extracted from the Prerogative Office in *Doctors-Commons*. The Second Edition. Price stich'd 1 s.

Memoirs of the DUTCH TRADE in all the States, Empires, and Kingdoms in the World. Shewing its first Rise and amazing Progress: After what Manner the DUTCH manage and carry on their Commerce; their vast Dominions and Government in the *Indies*, and by what Means they have made themselves Masters of all the Trade of EUROPE. As also what Goods and Merchandize are proper for Maritime Traffick, whence they are to be had, and what Gain and Profit they produce. A TREATISE very neecessary for every ENGLISHMAN. *Translated from the* French, *now Printed at* Amsterdam. By Mr. *Samber*. The Second Edition.

BOOKS

BOOKS

Sold by W. MEARS, *at the* Lamb *without* Temple-Bar.

A Survey of Trade. In Four Parts. I. The great Advantages of our Trade in General, and the Particular Influence of it on *Great-Britain*. II. The Marks of a beneficial Trade, and the Nature of our Commerce in its several Branches; with an Examination of some Notions generally received of the Prejudices we suffer by other Nations in Trade. III. The great Advantages of our *Colonies* and *Plantations* to *Great-Britain*, and our Interest in Preserving and Encouraging *Them*; and how *They* may be farther Improved. IV. Some Considerations on the Disadvantages our Trade at present labours under, and for the *Recovery* and *Enlargement* of it; of the *Assiento* Contract; of our Trade to *Spain*, &c. Together with Considerations on our Money and Bullion. Its Exportation discuss'd. Scarcity of Silver Coin accounted for. The Means of procuring a Plenty and Free Circulation of both Species. The Second Edition. Price. 5 s.

The Laws of *Jamaica*, pass'd by the Governours, Council and Assembly, in that Island, and confirm'd by the Crown. To which is prefix'd an Account of *Jamaica*. The Second Edition.

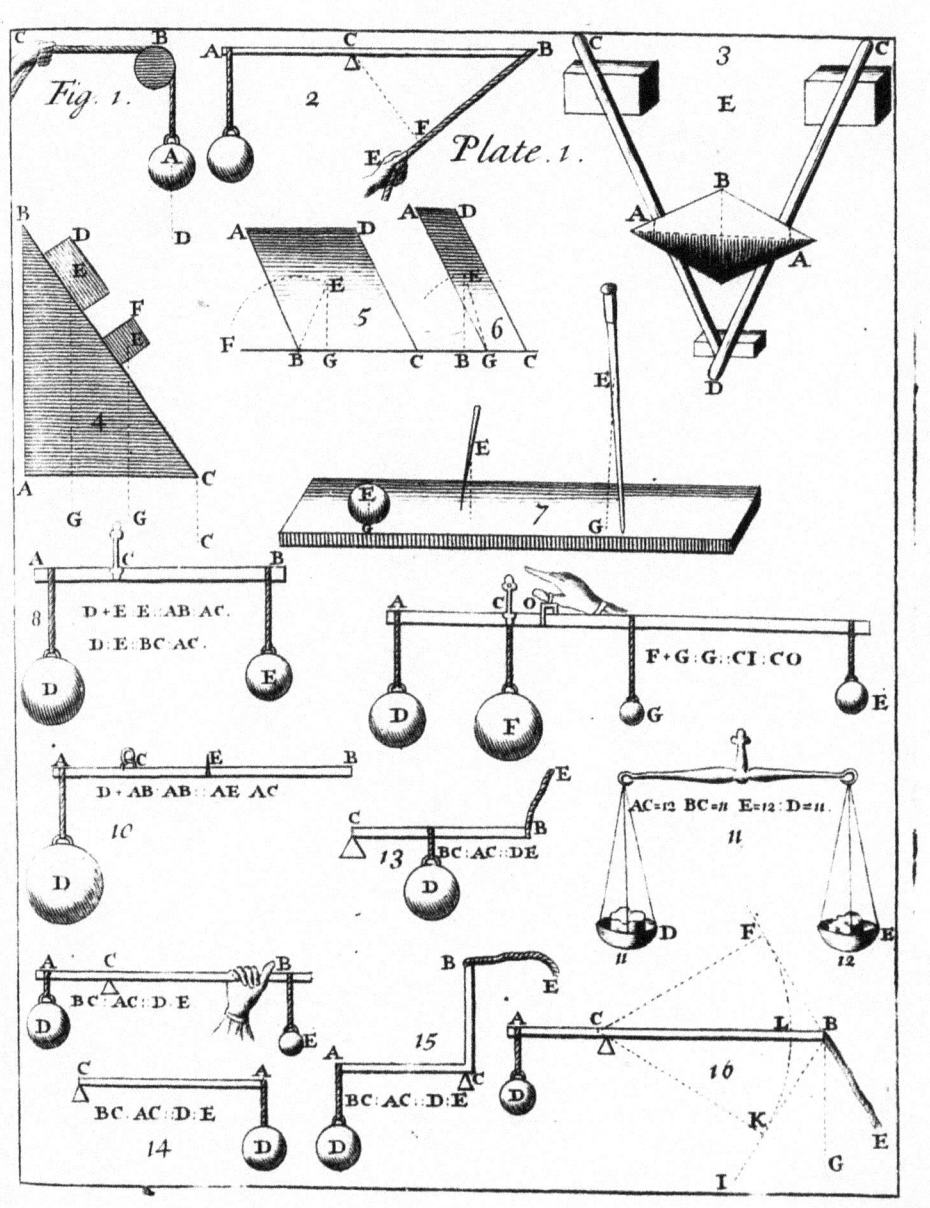

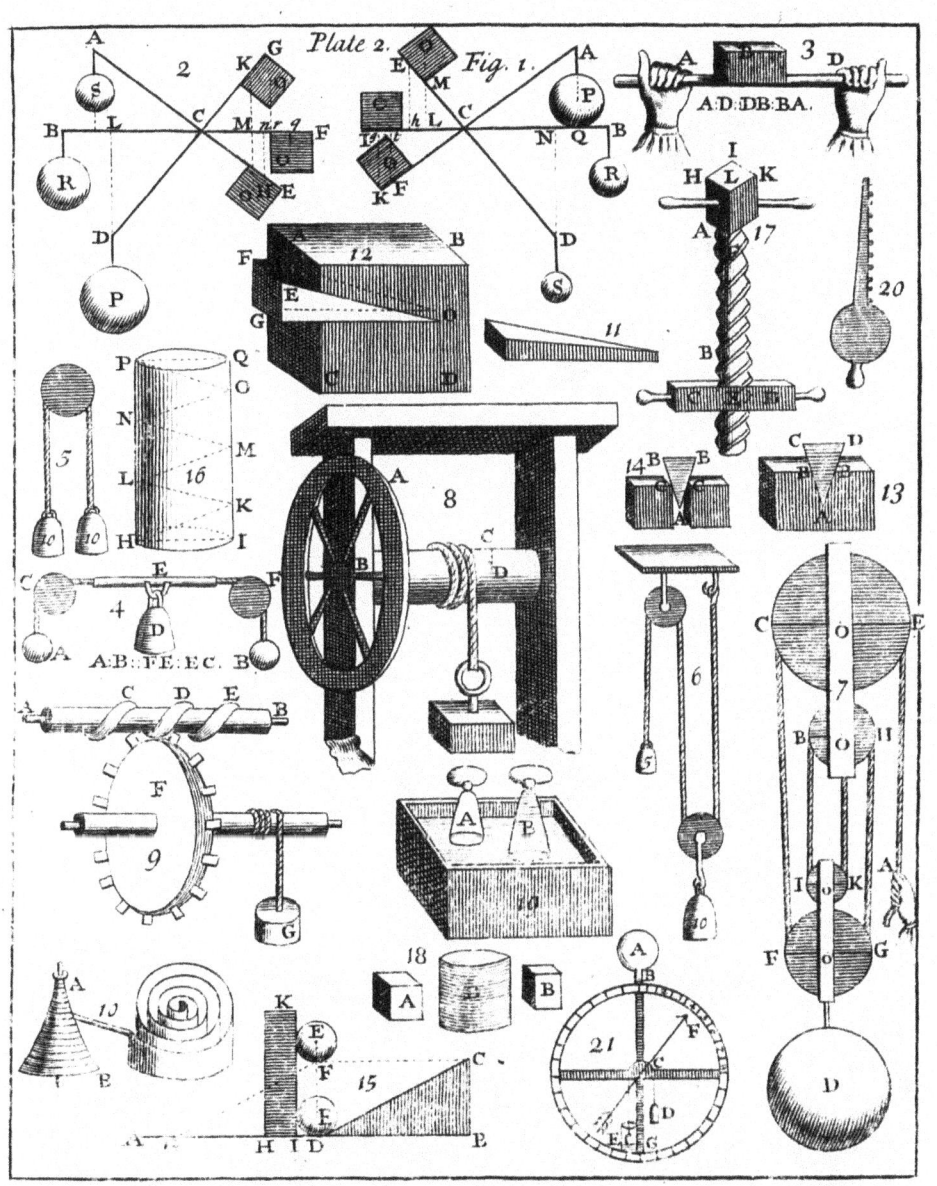

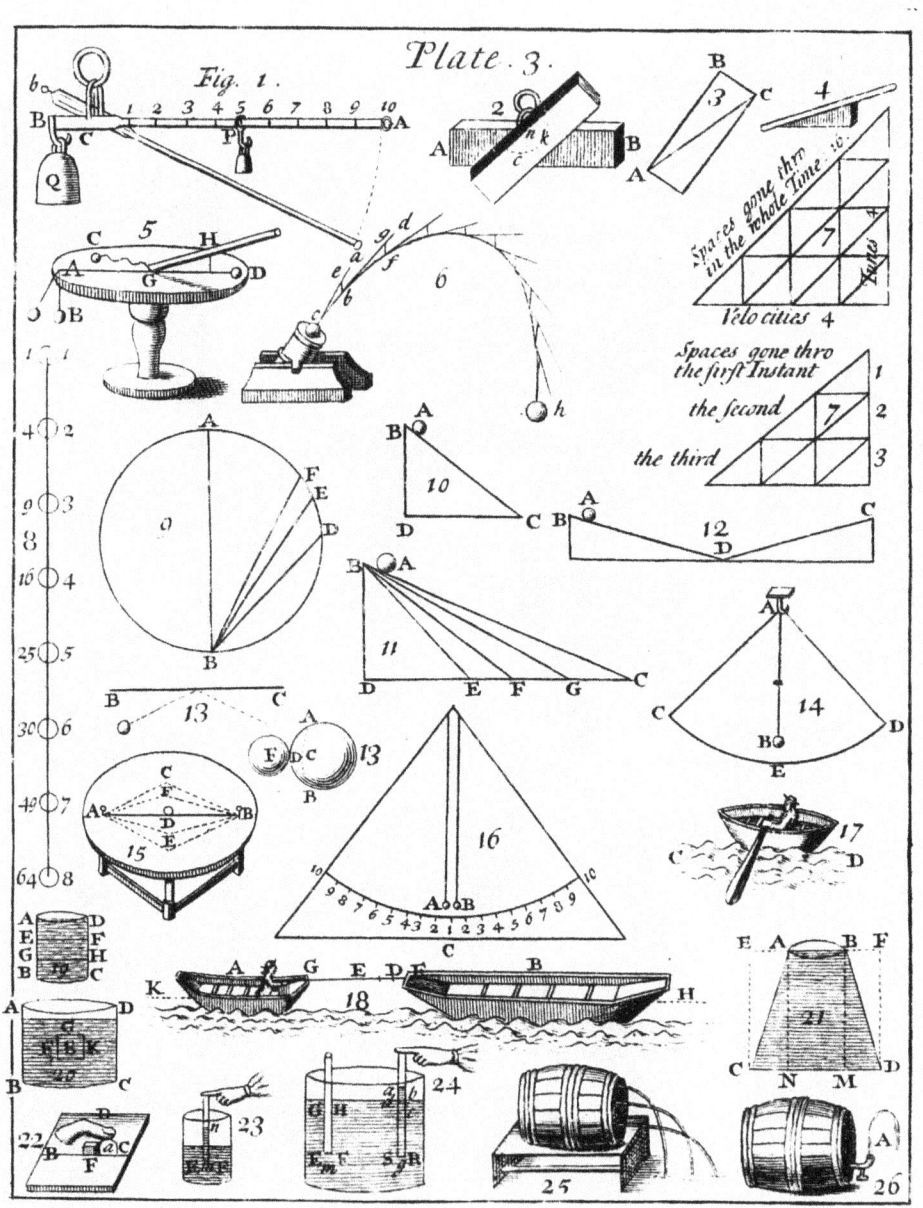

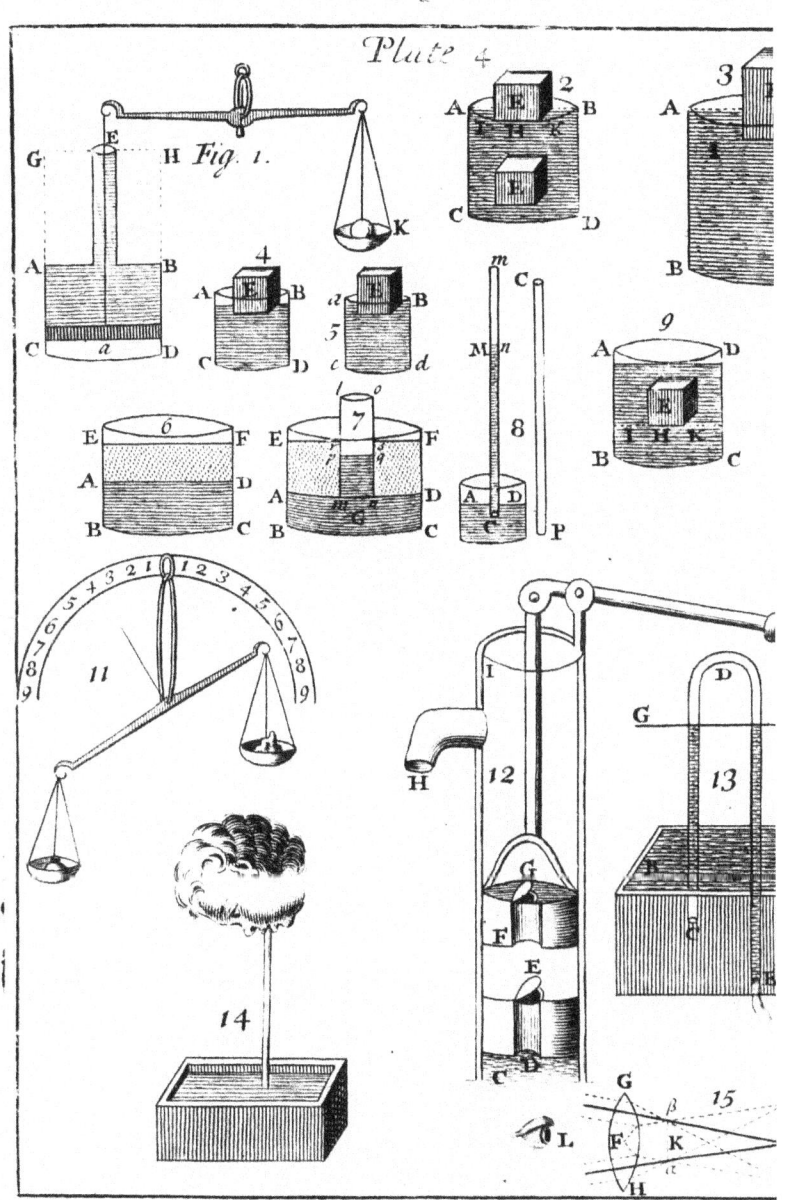

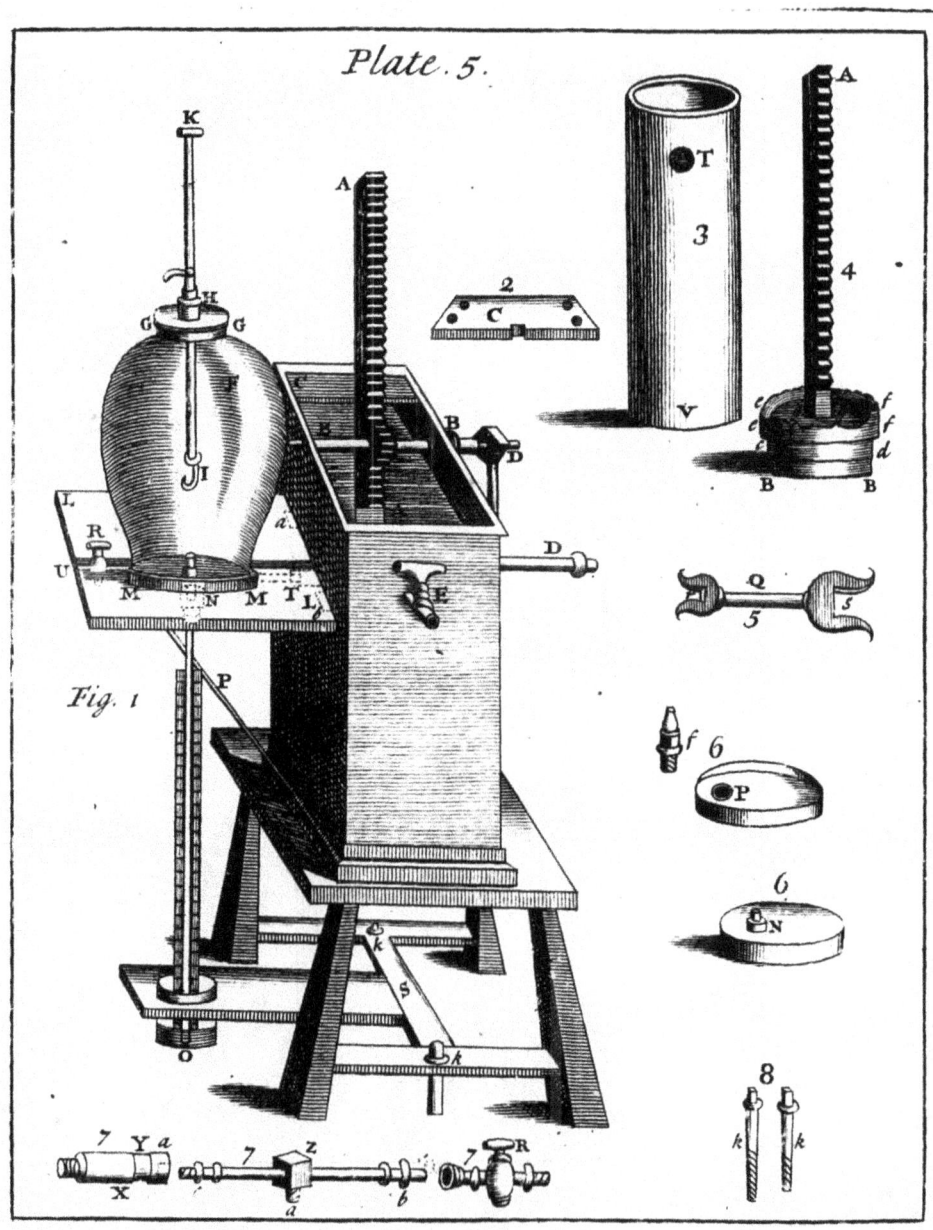

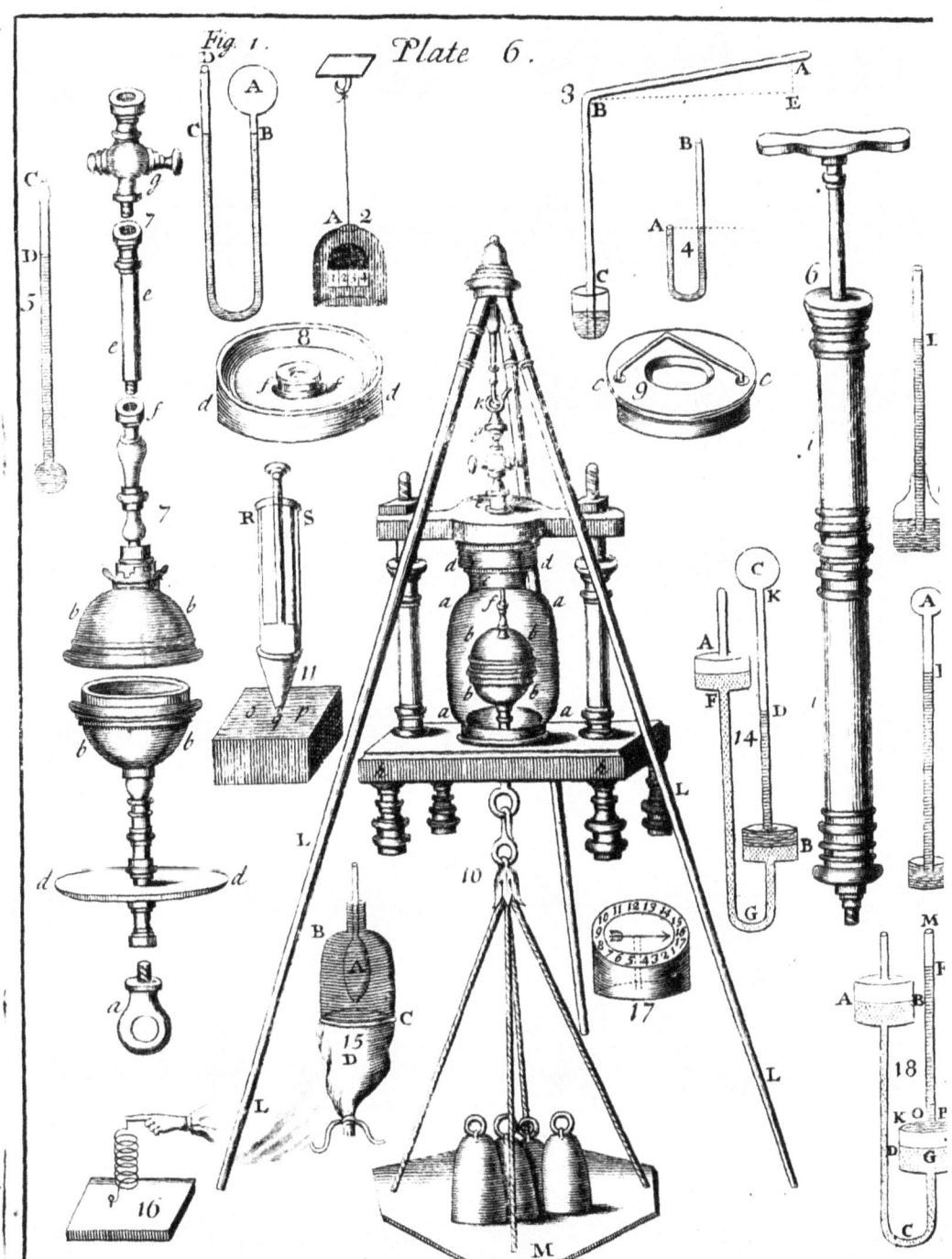
Plate 6.

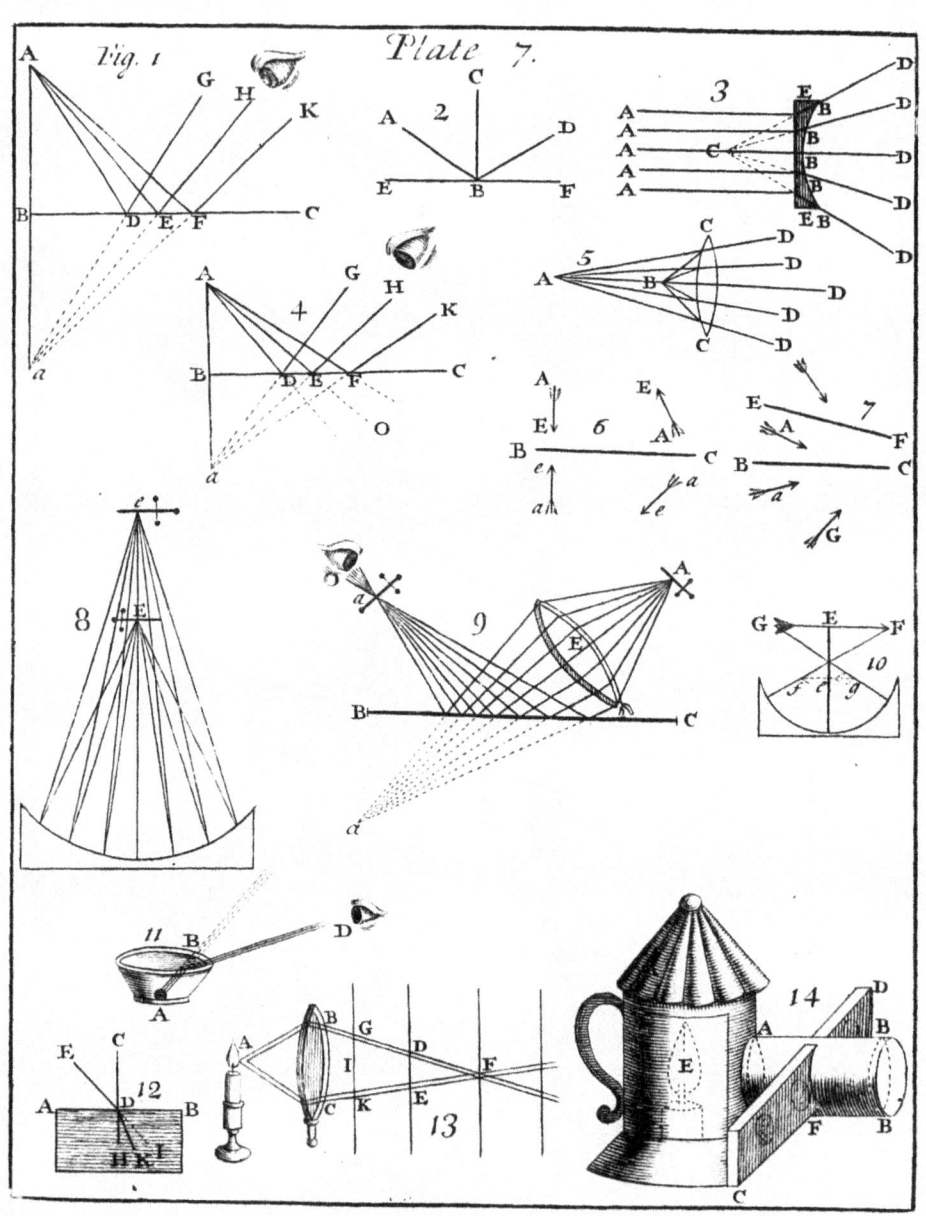

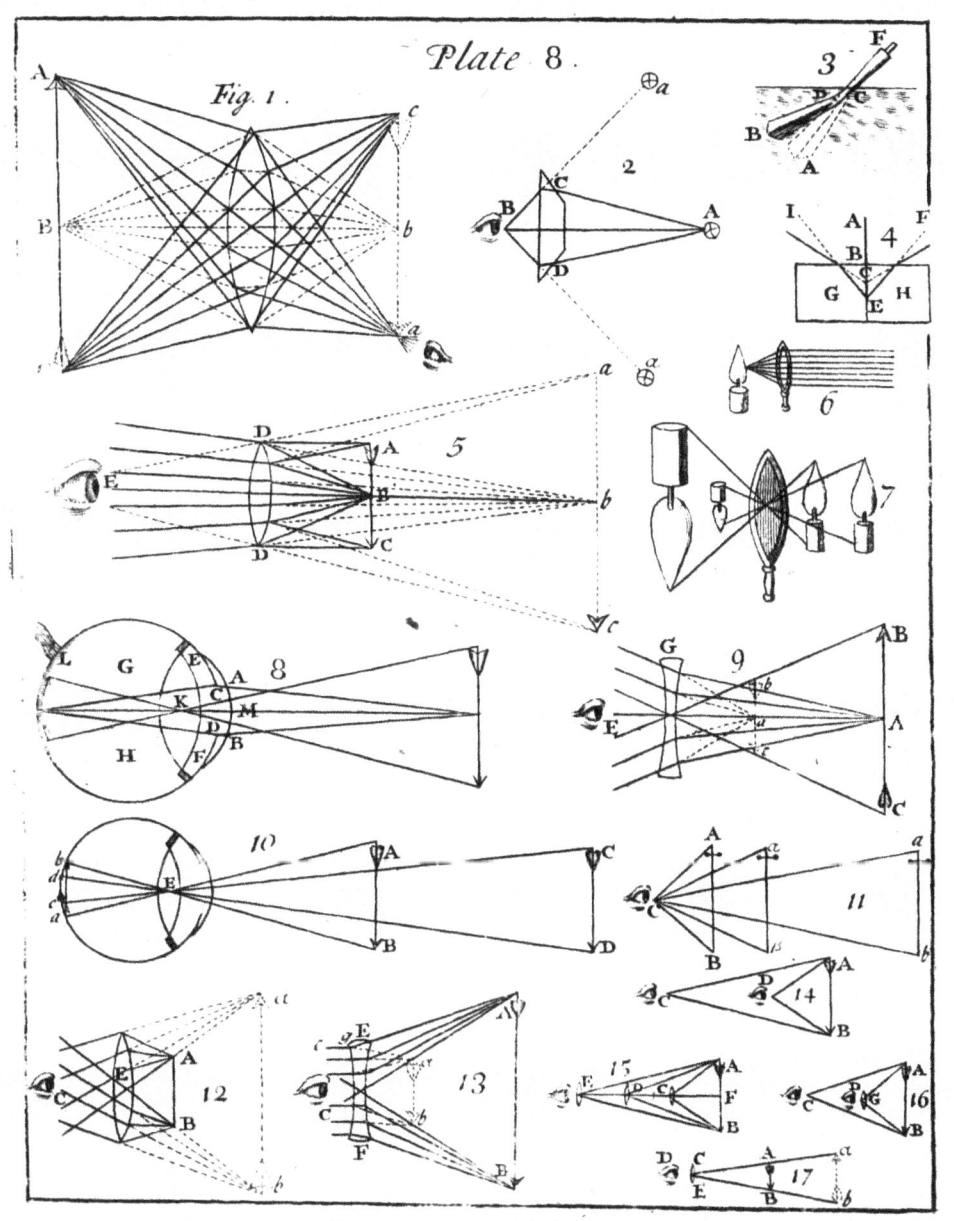

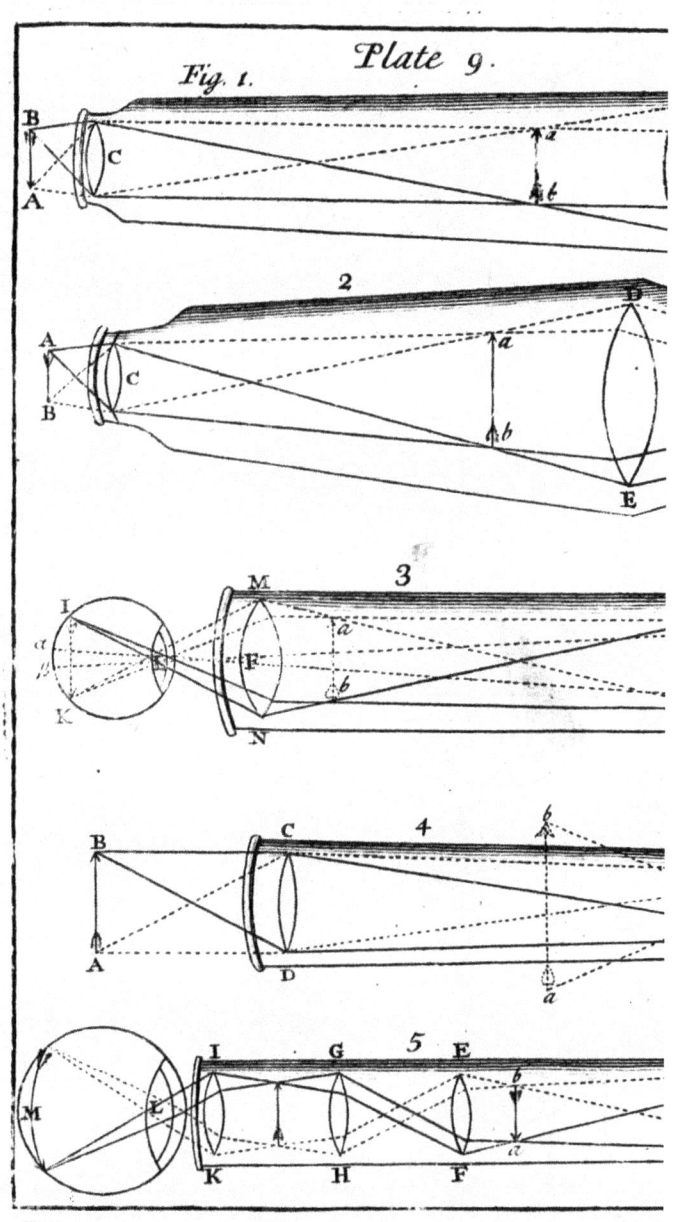

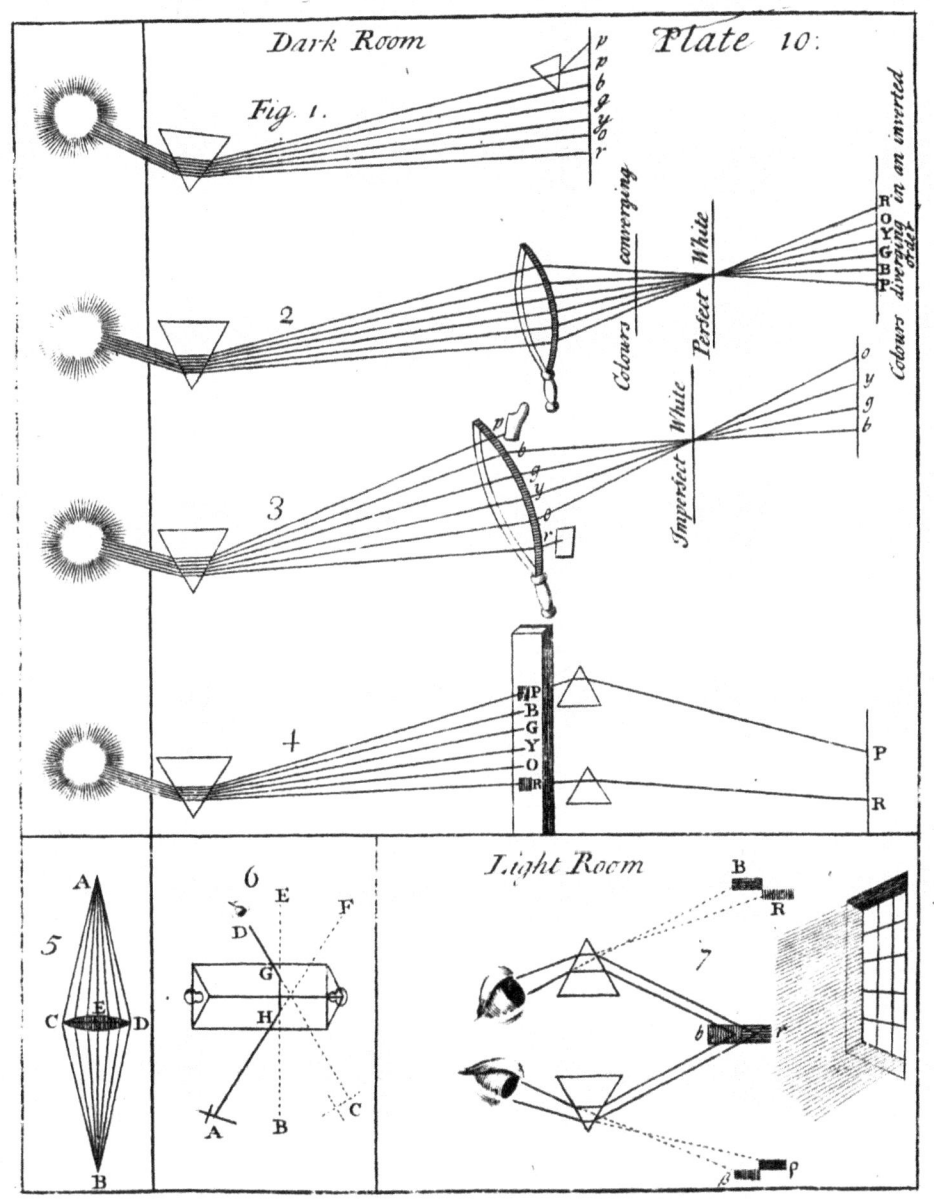

www.ingramcontent.com/pod-product-compliance
Lightning Source LLC
Chambersburg PA
CBHW080434110426
42743CB00016B/3168